ANCIENT &
MEDIEVAL
MODELLING

OSPREY MASTERCLASS

ANCIENT & MEDIEVAL
MODELLING

Pete Armstrong

© 2000 Osprey Publishing Limited

First published in 2000
by Osprey Publishing,
Elms Court, Chapel Way,
Botley, Oxford OX2 9LP, UK

Editor: Martin Windrow
Design: Frank Ainscough/Compendium
Printed through World Print Ltd, Hong Kong
00 01 02 03 04   10 9 8 7 6 5 4 3 2 1

FOR A CATALOGUE OF ALL TITLES
PUBLISHED BY OSPREY MILITARY,
MODELLING, AUTOMOTIVE AND AVIATION
PLEASE WRITE TO:

The Marketing Manager,
Osprey Direct,
PO Box 140,
Wellingborough,
Northants NN8 4ZA, United Kingdom
Email: info@OspreyDirect.co.uk

The Marketing Manager,
Osprey Direct USA,
PO Box 130,
Sterling Heights,
MI 48311-0130
USA
Email: info@OspreyDirectUSA.com

Or visit the Osprey website at:
http://www.osprey-publishing.co.uk

A CIP catalogue record of this book
is available from the British Library

ISBN 1 84176 007 2

CONTENTS

INTRODUCTION

ABOVE A startled cavegirl - my earliest surviving model, though I think I may still have 'Superboy's dog' somewhere...

This is a book about modelling; and although it includes a good deal of information about a variety of other relevant topics, it remains essentially a practical manual of techniques and modelling methods. My intention is not to attempt to cover every aspect of this large subject exhaustively, but rather to provide a basis on which the individual modeller can build through his own modelling experience and research.

Many of the topics touched upon in these pages - such as the evolution of armour, heraldry, ancient shield designs or medieval helmet crests - are subjects which would repay more extensive research. In many cases they are covered in other books, so my presentation of these and other fascinating subjects is styled as a sample 'taster', for the modeller to follow up for himself. He will find a number of starting points listed in the Bibliography.

My title, *Ancient and Medieval Modelling*, far from being restrictive, presents a vast span of history from which to chose subject matter; in fact it presents such a wealth of choice that it is inevitable that I have left out someone's favourite hobbyhorse. In reality, of course, the boundaries of any subject are only the boundaries of ones imagination. In seeking subjects from the ancient world we can look

RIGHT 'Richard Plantagenet, last of the English kings of England'. The author's 80mm model depicts the final moments of England's 'Black Legend' at Bosworth Field on 22 August 1485.

back as far as the Old Stone Age if we choose – I've always had a soft spot for troglodytes since Aurora brought out a rather startled cavewoman in dire need of rescue in the early days of my interest in modelling. I was probably still at school when Airfix produced a model of the Black Prince in 1:12 scale, and I'm sure they made a Joan of Arc too. I was a voracious consumer of plastic kits in those days, and I made them both in a day; they were my earliest essays in medieval modelling and, not surprisingly, they have not survived.

My perspective on history derives from an Anglo-Saxon standpoint, so I have always considered that the withdrawal of the Roman Legions from Britain and the sack of Rome by Alaric the Goth in 410 AD signified the onset of the 'Dark Ages', and that Duke William of Normandy's conquest of England in 1066 heralded the beginning of the 'medieval' centuries. The academic purist would debate that common perception; but few would dispute that the 'Middle Ages' came to an end with the death in battle of Richard Plantagenet, last of the English kings of England, at Bosworth in 1485.

In Scotland the line is rather less clear-cut: it would not do for modellers of the medieval period to exclude the last great battle fought between the English and Scots nations at Flodden in 1513. In military terms the battle of Flodden could belong to the previous century; it was a medieval afterthought, fought in the age of the Tudors. King James IV of Scotland, along with a quarter of his army and the flower

of the Scots nobility, lay dead on the field of battle as nightfall brought the great clash of armies to a close – surely as dramatic a conclusion to the Middle Ages as any modeller seeking powerful subject matter could wish for.

FORM & CONTENT

Each of the following chapters has as its core an illustrated step-by-step description detailing the construction of a model. My original intention was to grade the difficulties and levels of skill progressively through the chapters, but this has not always been strictly possible. The best that can be said is that the medieval subjects progress from a fairly simple project to a large and involved model which includes buildings, figures and a multitude of accessories. I had also intended to follow chronological order, but the difficulties of making this mesh with a logical progression of technical challenges defeated me; my Anglo-Saxon warrior and Roman trooper will be found in the rearguard.

To prevent repetition in the text, those modelling techniques which recur in several chapters are discussed in full in the technical section of Chapter 1, and readers are referred back to this chapter from various points in the text.

The step-by-step core of each chapter is supported by relevant drawings and photographic reference material. When possible I have included the work of some of my associates who produce medieval models to

ABOVE The Florentine modeller Mario Venturi interprets and models the death of Richard III quite differently and in his own individual style in this 54mm vignette.

further illustrate and expand on the subject matter of the featured project. My criteria in selecting illustrations has been to avoid as far as possible pictures of familiar stock figures assembled and painted 'straight from the box'. I have chosen instead to illustrate models which display the creative imagination and technical expertise of their authors. The great majority of the photographs and drawings that follow have been produced especially for this book and have not been published previously.

The models featured in the step-by-step sections of the book are not designed as patterns or plans to be copied rigidly, but serve rather as vehicles for describing modelling methods; I hope they will stimulate the reader's imagination and provide starting points from which individual modellers can develop in their own directions.

Although the book is not a guide to scratch-building figures it does advocate a creative approach to modelling, and seeks to encourage readers to incorporate as much of their own craftsmanship and ideas into their modelling projects as possible. I have used commercially available figure kits and accessories from my own 'Border Miniatures' range as the basis of most of the modelling projects; the exceptions are noted and credited. The kits are treated as the craftsman's raw materials, to be developed imaginatively, rather than as an end in themselves to be painted without any further creative input. The modelling process, by which I mean the activity before any painting takes place, forms a large part of my subject matter. My themes are essentially military though I have tried to include a brief consideration of other amusing, interesting or potentially fruitful directions.

To add interest and variety to the figure modelling projects I have used a range of ancient and medieval settings for figures, such as a castle courtyard, Hadrian's Wall in the wilds of Northumbria, and the battlefield. Most of the figures I have used are 80mm size; this enables a great deal of detail to be incorporated into the models and allows scope for the inclusion of a multitude of interesting accessories, extensive groundwork and parts of buildings, even when a mounted figure is included. The finished projects are part scale-model and part three-dimensional illustration, for as well as depicting arms, armour and costume as exactly as possible there is also a dramatic element present, which infuses life into the models.

Pete Armstrong
Keswick
July 1999

RIGHT The Northumbrian modeller Keith Durham knows the evocative battlefield of Flodden well, and has turned to it for inspiration for this 'English Billman of 1513'.

FAR RIGHT A dramatic incident unfolds in the castle courtyard as the Earl of Warwick's cat trots home with an offering for his master... Taking the time to add a detail like this can bring instant life to a model which may otherwise be technically excellent but a little 'stiff'.

CHAPTER 1

TOOLS, MATERIALS & TECHNIQUES

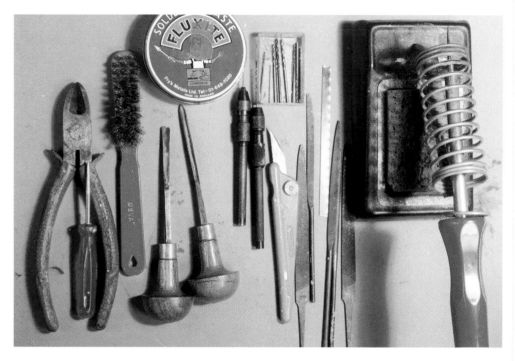

LEFT A selection of the small hand tools that I use most frequently. Unfortunately I didn't have room to include my favourite hacksaw and piercing saw; but readers with a fascination for pictures of saws and the like will find some exciting tool catalogues listed in Appendix A.

SMALL HAND TOOLS

The choice of small hand tools - files, cutting blades, pliers and tweezers, etc - is always a matter of personal preference, and it is unlikely that any two modellers' workbenches would display the exactly same assortment. The only rule is to buy the best quality that you can afford. Cheap tools are a false economy, and will always have to be replaced sooner rather than later; the cost of two or three Chinese-made tools will soon add up to more than that of one European or American one.

In the middle of my modelling desk are clustered the tools that are used most frequently. Most are simple and inexpensive, and some are home-made. There are very few tools that are exclusive to model making; they all have other uses, so they must be jealously guarded from predators. Cluttering drawers within easy reach are tools which are sometimes useful; the less-often used lie gathering dust on shelves in the workshop. There are even tools which are never used at all, some of them mystifying puzzles which must have seemed a good idea at the time. Then there are those which were presents from the well-meaning, and the broken gadgets and tools blunted in the last outbreak of decorating fever; they might come in handy sometime.

A most useful recent addition to my work desk is a variable speed Expo Mini-Drill. I was rather sceptical about its usefulness at first, but I wouldn't be without it now. I use it for practically all drilling and grinding and for buffing and polishing work. These are powerful little machines which - with the right safety precautions in place - can also be used to make small turned components from brass rod. To do this the Mini-Drill should be clamped firmly to the desk, preferably under a magnifying lamp which will not only light the work but provide essential eye protection. Short lengths of brass rod up to about 4mm in diameter can be held in the chuck and turned to shape using various needle files. It is surprising how quickly previously elusive shapes can be made by this simple method.

Just as individual as the selection of tools is the way in which they are used. Techniques can be employed in a personal manner, and they are described here from that viewpoint; readers should regard this chapter as a starting point on which to build their own practical experience.

At several points in the text you will note that I have recourse to my 'scrapbox' for parts.

This is really a variety of boxes, trays and drawers where I have amassed a vast array of bits and pieces that 'might come in useful sometime'. There are boxes of brass rods and etched frets, jewellery chain, landscaping materials, balsa, plywood and card, and a whole tray of parts left over from plastic and white metal kits.

RIGHT The construction of this soldered brass weather vane is described in detail in Chapter 5. The flat brass has been cut to shape and soldered on to a brass pole, tapered by using my Mini-Drill as an improvised lathe. The finial is made from the top of a sword hilt found in the scrapbox.

SOLDERING - EQUIPMENT & METHODS

Soldering has advantages over glueing when working with metals, as it forms a strong joint instantly. The only piece of equipment needed is a 15 watt electric soldering iron, which will provide enough heat for most jobs; however, a soldering torch can be useful too. The iron should have a metal stand in which it can rest safely during a soldering session; these usually have an integral sponge in a tray below the holder, which is kept damp to wipe any build-up of unwanted solder off the bit. You need a tin of Fluxite, which is an effective general-purpose flux in paste form well suited to the uncomplicated work described here.

No other specialised tools are needed: only an assortment of files, a small brass-bristled brush, and several craft knives to use as scrapers and to help position blobs of flux. As there are numerous references to soldering throughout this book it seems worthwhile to consider the basic method in this section. Other, more specialised applications will be described later as they crop up in the modelling projects.

Very low temperature solder such as Carr's No.70 is used to assemble white metal components; it melts at 70 degrees C, but when fused with white metal it re-melts at a higher temperature and so forms a very secure bond. A solder with a higher melting point is needed in cases when working with brass. A general purpose resin-cored solder which melts at about 180 degrees C is ideal for this, and is available in handy coil form on a reel from any ironmonger.

Start by practising soldering scraps of white metal together before you embark on the castings themselves. The description of my methods below should give modellers some help, but there is nothing to beat hands-on experience for developing skills. Be selective, too, in what you attempt - there are situations where glue is a better option, particularly when large flat surfaces need to be joined.

Soft solders not only form joins; they also act as fillers, which can be useful when working on armoured figures. Any blemishes on the surface of the plates can be filled with a blob of solder which when tidied up will blend perfectly into the metal of the casting.

The copper soldering iron bit should be pointed for our purposes, and this means filing it to shape - commercial bits always seem to be chisel-ended. A pointed bit will enable you to pick up tiny particles of solder of the exact size needed, and place them precisely where needed on the work in progress.

To make a joint with low temperature solder between two small white metal components, first scrape the surfaces to be joined back to bright metal with a craft knife; this removes any oxydisation from the surface which might inhibit the flow of the solder and prevent it fusing with the metal. The surfaces to be joined will need to be held firmly together before they are soldered; however, given the low temperature involved, I usually contrive a way of positioning one part with bits of Plastilene, so that I can hold the other part against it with my fingers. With my free hand I use a knife blade to pick up some flux and place it on the join where the solder is intended to run. Just enough solder to do the job is then picked up on the bit of the iron, and placed on the fluxed joint, where it will run

and fuse the parts together. There is unlikely to be enough heat in this operation to burn your fingers.

If, as is often the case, the copper bit refuses to pick up the solder, then it needs cleaning – first with the sponge, then lightly with a fine file, after which it should be quickly dipped in the flux.

The heat should at all times be applied to the solder; take care not to bring the iron in contact with the castings, or they will melt; use a light touch, and do not 'dwell' with the iron.

Once the brass is tinned in this way, the next stage is to coat it with very low temperature solder. Clean and flux the tinned area; then bring a blob of Carr's No.70 solder to the work on the tip of the bit; as the brass is heated with the iron this will flow over the previously applied higher-melt solder and fuse with it.

The contact surface of the white metal part should now be cleaned, fluxed, and held firmly in position. Use very low temperature solder to form the join, as described above. (Remember, be careful: although heat can be ꞏ ꞏ d to the solder and to the tinned brass ꞏse the joint, it is important ꞏ t heat to the white metal, or ꞏ this method, for instance, ꞏr heads can be soldered to ꞏ brass locating rods can be ꞏetal components.

ꞏLLING PUTTIES

ꞏ putty – which I refer to ꞏ the popular brand name ꞏout this book – is a familiar ꞏd medium of which most ꞏve experience. It is practically ꞏavoid using Milliput, and ꞏthat it finds a wide variety of ꞏhroughout the projects ꞏre are several grades of ꞏe, but I have never found that ꞏ offer any real advantage over ꞏrade which I invariably use. ꞏfigures I prefer to work as far ꞏctly in metal. This confers

form the classic ring mail for which we have direct physical evidence.

Mail shirts are heavy - those in the Wallace Collection in London weigh up to 19lbs (9 kilos) - and mail will try to hang vertically at all times. The links are small, less than a half-inch (10mm) in diameter, so visually some shirts made of very fine links appear almost to have the texture of a woollen fabric. Even so, always remember that mail does not cling to the body unless it is lying on a horizontal surface - it is always trying to escape any confinement in order to hang vertically. On an actual mail-clad arm held out parallel to the ground the linked rings along the top surface will 'stare' as far apart as the construction allows; down the sides the rings will behave like water, seeking the lowest level, and unless the sleeve is very tight-fitting it will 'bag' along the bottom surface.

The best that can be achieved in model form is an impression of these tens of thousands of links; we need a texture that serves as a visual equivalent to what we see in real life. There are ways of modelling mail with fine wire wrapped round a former and cut into links (the same way that real mail was produced), or simply flattened as a coil. However, a less tedious method using Milliput provides an acceptable solution. All you need is a steady hand, a magnifier and a simple, home-made mail-making tool. Mine is fashioned from a small hypodermic needle which the vet was kind enough to supply last time he looked at the dog. The hollow needle is cut at an angle and filed to shape so that it produces a U-shaped impression when pressed into modelling putty. A row of these shapes is pressed into the putty horizontally, moving in one direction; then a row going the opposite way is impressed immediately underneath the first, which makes a series of S-shapes. The third row reverses direction again and similarly joins with the row above to further develop the pattern - and so on, *ad* very nearly *infinitum...*

An instance of the need to model an area of mail occurs in Chapter 3 when, in the process of repositioning a mail-clad arm, I am left with a gap that needs to be made good. Milliput was pressed firmly into place and shaped to replace the missing section of the arm. Only when the putty begins to harden a little should the mail-maker be used to create the texture. At the painting stage thin black paint is flooded into the detail of the mail, but only the Milliput section will need a light touch of silver paint to match it with the metal of the casting. A later coat of varnish should serve to further unify the arm.

ABOVE Sculpture in 80mm showing a detail of mail modelled using the method described; the manner in which the 'U-tool' has been used can be clearly seen. Despite the fact that I prefer to work directly in metal, textures such as mail have to be added with modelling putty – it would be absurd not to take advantage of the versatility of this material.

some definite advantages with armoured figures, as the metal used can be burnished to represent the surface quality of armour. Modelling putty needs to be painted to achieve a metallic effect, and this is not always easy. However, there are instances when there is no alternative to its use, and modelling mail armour is such a case.

MODELLING MAIL ARMOUR

Most medieval modellers will be familiar with the manner in which mail is constructed from interlocked and riveted wire rings. There are theories - hotly debated - which stem from the interpretation of medieval drawings and sculpture as suggesting that several varieties existed, such as 'banded' and 'solid' mail. However, I leave this vexed subject to the experts; my concern is representing in model

Larger areas of mail can be built up in a similar manner; if a complete mail shirt is undertaken then waistbelts, baldrics or shield-carrying straps may conveniently subdivide the shirt into manageable areas which can be tackled in stages. If an area of mail is too large to model in one session or if the Milliput hardens before the texturing work is finished, then a join needs to be contrived at the start of the next session. The join between the completed area and the next section is best made on the line of a vertical column of links; it may be necessary to cut away some of the complete work to achieve this.

PAINTING

An outline in this chapter of the painting methods and materials that I have used throughout the book will save much repetition later.

Light is the first essential to consider before paints and brushes are given any thought. Ideally I would always work in bright daylight next to a window, but in reality most of my painting is done under artificial light with the help of a magnifying lamp. Daylight simulation bulbs give a cold blue light rather than the warm glow of tungsten lighting. Provided that the finished model is displayed in the same lighting conditions as those in which it was painted I can see little advantage in the former.

Decent brushes are essential; I go through sheaves of them - they don't last long. It doesn't matter whether they are sable or synthetic, so long as the brushes used for fine work come to a point and stay that way, and the ones used for broader work don't shed their hair.

I use Humbrol Matt Enamels as the basis for all my painting. I supplement these with Artists Oil Colours, which I add to the enamel in small amounts. The oil colours are used simply to make up for deficiencies in the colour range that modellers' enamels offer. Matt white enamel is the basis of all my colour mixing; in addition I use matt black and the primary colours - scarlet, yellow and blue. Gloss varnish is useful to give a shiny finish over matt paint and to seal and give depth to burnished armour; the Humbrol range metallics, gold and silver, are also invaluable. Probably the most useful oil colours which supplement the primaries are Crimson Lake, Yellow Ochre and Ultramarine. Enamels are particularly weak in earth colours, but oils make good this deficiency, providing us with Burnt and Raw varieties of Umber and Sienna.

I always thin paints with real turpentine, which helps paint to dry. In my experience turps substitute should never be mixed with paint, as it imparts a dull, lifeless surface quality and impedes drying; it should only be used for cleaning brushes.

Though I discuss relevant aspects of painting in each chapter I have not included any step-by-step accounts of painting figures in this book. I have assumed that the reader is not a complete newcomer to modelling, and if he is then there are a number of books on the market which will tell him all he needs to know (e.g. see Bibliography, *Bill Horan's Military Modelling Masterclass*). Nor have I bothered you with tedious tales of the times my matt paint dried with a shiny gloss finish, nor mentioned what I said when the matt varnish turned white in the incised detail. (Incidentally, a remedy for the latter mishap is to bin the offending tin and buy a fresh one...)The heraldry section following Chapter 4 contains advice regarding the correct colours to use for 'gules' and the other heraldic 'tinctures'.

HERALDIC TRANSFERS

Transfers (decals) offer a simple way of overcoming the difficulties of painting heraldry - particularly repeated images - on shields, surcoats and banners. The reluctance on the part of many figure modellers to use transfers is not shared by aircraft or vehicle modellers, who use them as a matter of course. Waterslide transfers are readily available and versatile, and modellers of all abilities will find it useful to

ABOVE Shields displaying the coats of arms of six famous 14th century French knights are illustrated here. The background colour has been painted on the shield in gloss finish; then a heraldic transfer from my own range has been used to add the designs.

have a few around. There are a few technical points to observe in order to get the best results.

In all cases the transfers must be applied to a gloss surface. This is because a matt finish is by definition rough and uneven, absorbing light to produce the matt effect, and the transfer will not adhere to this. Quite the opposite is true of a flat reflective gloss finish; so it may be necessary to gloss varnish some parts of the model before putting the transfer in place.

Transfers can prove reluctant to conform to the curved surfaces of shields and can be particularly difficult to persuade to take up the shape of the folds in a surcoat. In these cases you should resort to Transfer Softener. A bottle of this solution should put even the most reticent of transfers in its place; simply read the instructions on the label, and use it generously. When all is in position and dry a coat of thin gloss varnish will fix the transfer permanently in place. You can then either give the transfer a coat of matt varnish to blend it in with the rest of the model; or you can use it as a guide and hand-paint the design over it.

This not only disguises the fact that you have used a transfer, but also allows you to change the colours and make other simple adjustments. A little creative brushwork could add a heraldic difference such as a bordure or a label, and could crown a lion or add a second tail. From the starting point of a simple transfer there are many possibilities.

BURNISHING & POLISHING ARMOUR

White metal castings can be burnished and buffed so that the surface of the metal takes on the quality of plate armour or a weapon blade. In fact anything which needs to look realistically metallic can be treated in this way, from large areas of plate armour down to sword blades, belt buckles and buttons. The method is essentially simple but rather tedious; here is how you should proceed.

First brush the casting over with a soft brass-bristled brush such as those sold in shoe shops for cleaning suede. This will bring the casting up to a bright shine, but will still leave visible scratch marks. Removing these is the crucial part of the operation. The armoured part of the casting is burnished with the side of a blunt needle or similar hard steel tool, which is worked over the surface of the casting with a circular motion, taking care to use a light touch to create a smooth, even, bright surface. Each separate plate of the armour is treated in this way individually, taking care not to remove rivets and other fine detail.

If the figure is in full plate armour - particularly if this is e.g. highly decorated Maximilian armour of the late 15th century - then this can seem as time-consuming as the chores of the servants who had to polish the real thing. Recently I have been using my Mini-Drill to experiment with ways of speeding up this process; I feel sure that my new machine can be used to burnish the plates, but as yet my results are uneven. The drill works well at the brass-brushing stage and is good for final buffing of the armour, but at the moment I still feel that burnishing the plates by hand gives more control over the process and achieves the best results.

The casting should now be smooth and bright - in fact it may be rather too bright. Unless you are representing a tournament or other 'parade' scenario, when 'white' armours were often polished to a mirror finish, it needs to be toned down and finished to represent the slightly dulled surface of armour as worn on campaign. Thin black paint is flooded over the casting, then wiped off; this should dull the armour slightly and leave a residue to outline the individual plates and fittings. When this is dry the outlining can be touched up, and highlights on the armour can be polished up a little with a paper towel. Two or three coats of thin varnish, slightly tinted to darken it, are used finally to finish the armour with a deep translucent sheen.

Areas of mail armour are easier and quicker to deal with than plate. Mail need not be burnished as this would destroy the delicate detail. Simply brush the mail to a bright shine with a brass-bristled brush, then flood thin black paint into the detail. When this is dry the mail is given the lightest of touches over with a finger to highlight the detail, and then varnished as described above.

These methods can also be used, with variation, to represent yellow metals such as brass, bronze and copper. The castings are initially burnished to a bright shine, but then colour needs to be introduced into the varnish used to finish the process to achieve the effect of a rich yellow metal. The key to this lies in retaining a translucent surface, and in avoiding the rather lifeless effect which results when opaque metallic paint is used. To get this translucent effect a succession of light tinted layers of varnish should be applied carefully, so as to build up a metallic sheen without quite obscuring the underlying burnished metal. The pigments used to tint the varnish need to be as finely ground as possible, to avoid the granular surface quality associated with metallic paints. Metallic printer's ink has been used successfully in this context, as well as various coloured drawing inks and mixtures of coloured pigment and metallic powders. Successful yellow metal effects are more difficult to achieve than white metal, and there is a good deal of scope for experimentation in this area.

SIZE & SCALE

My concern in these pages is with figures sized from 54mm up to 120mm; between these extremes lie a wide range of sizes and scales which offer a good deal of potential to the creative modeller. The larger end of this range are more suited to vignettes, small groupings

and for presentation as single figures. Generally figures below 54mm tend to belong in the realm of the AFV enthusiast (1/35 scale or 52mm), or the wargamer, who tends to prefer 25mm and smaller. Wargames figures, particularly 25mm size, present interesting possibilities and are especially effective when used en masse to represent large formations of soldiers on the battlefield, perhaps incorporating buildings. Dioramas such as a scale model of a complete castle would similarly be brought to life by the inclusion of groups of these small figures. As to figures above 120mm, I'm sure that few modellers would disagree that though they may remain models they cease to have the charm of miniatures. I have never considered that the impact of a model should depend upon its size, and I'm sure that all a modeller needs to say can be said with figures well below 120mm.

It is sensible before starting a vignette or diorama model to work out the scale for any specific groundwork items or parts of buildings by using the size of the figures as a starting point. For instance, a 54mm figure represents a 6ft (1.83m) person without headgear, and this is represented as a scale by the ratio 1:34 (54x34 = 1836, i.e. near enough 1830mm, giving the scale 1:34). A 'standard scale' figure, as 1:32 scale is sometimes termed, will be 57mm high. Thus an 80mm figure is in 1:23 scale, a 90mm figure is 1:20 scale and a 120mm figure is 1:15 scale. A 150mm figure would be in 1:12 scale; this gives

RIGHT Drumcoltran Castle, a late medieval Scottish tower house in Kirkcudbrightshire, modelled as it stands today. The 'L'-shaped tower is a domestic fortification built on a modest scale, and proved an ideal subject to model in its entirety. A series of photographs and measurements were taken on site; these were developed into scale drawings from which the model was built. I used a linear scale of 4mm:1ft, so I was able to make the roof from sheets of 00 gauge plasticard tile mouldings from the model railway shop. Most of the building was made from thin wood sections and card. The window openings are filled with brass bird-repellent frets. (Author's model)

FAR RIGHT Author's scale drawing of Drumcoltran, worked up from a series of photos and measurements. The areas of stonework, particularly above windows and doors and the corner quoins, were drawn exactly, then the areas between were rendered in a more stylised manner.

a linear scale of 1in = 1ft - an easy scale to work in, and one generally used for dolls' houses, but with this scale we are moving outside the realm of the miniaturist.

A useful scale to choose if complete buildings are to be modelled is 1:72 or 4mm = 1ft, the linear scale of '00 gauge' model railways; figures are 24mm in height, and a wealth of useful accessories, building parts and figures are commercially available.

The simplest of several systems used by Renaissance artists for dividing the human

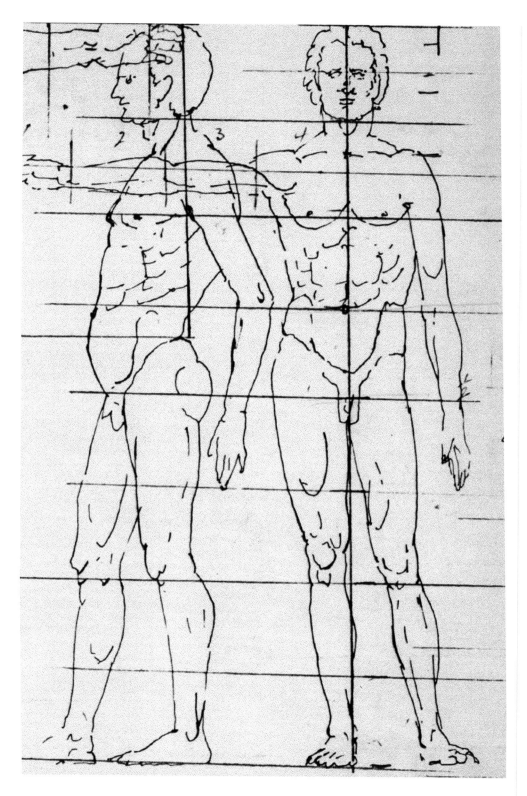

figure to clarify its proportions is that devised by Vitruvius and known to us from a drawing by Leonardo da Vinci. This system divides the figure into equal parts using the head as the module, and results in the classic figure of 'eight heads'. As the accompanying drawing shows, this provides a useful device to enable the modeller and converter to check the proportions of a miniature figure. If we apply this system to a 1:32 or 57mm figure we find that the head should measure 7mm. Similarly an 80mm figure's head would measure 10mm, and that of a 120mm figure would be 15mm. With Vitruvius' system as a tool, proportions need be less of a problem to figure modellers.

The proportions of horses do not divide up quite so neatly as does the human figure, but the Bibliography lists an invaluable *Atlas of Animal Anatomy* which provides a wealth of measured drawings of horses, dogs and other animals.

RESEARCH & FIELDWORK

FAR RIGHT A wealth of detail is captured in a corner of Aydon Castle, a fine 13th century fortified manor house in Northumberland. The carefully cut ashlar blocks of the battlements contrast with the more random stonework and inserted brick arch with its rustic quoins.

CENTRE RIGHT Areas of open ground such as a castle courtyard need to be made varied and interesting, and good reference material eases the modeller's problem. At Aydon the intimate scale of the buildings gives appeal. In this view, though the foreground is pure English Heritage, the surface of the courtyard beyond is broken by interesting undulating cobblestones and a pattern of paved paths. The modest gateway proved an ideal feature to incorporate into a model, and can be found in the inner courtyard of the castle modelled in Chapter 5.

RIGHT An interesting late medieval doorway at Naworth Castle in Cumbria with a rare surviving iron gate or 'yett' which still retains enough of its board infill to demonstrate how these doors were constructed. Iron yetts were a common feature of medieval fortified buildings on the Borders and in Scotland. The picture was taken without a model in mind at the time but turned out - see Chapter 5 - to be an invaluable source of inspiration.

Historical modelling aims to recreate in miniature people and scenes from the past in authentic detail. Though books will probably provide a main source of information, these can be supplemented by research in the field from first hand sources, to add a more original dimension to our work. Britain is fortunate that a wealth of her medieval-built heritage survives; remains from earlier times are less obvious and demand a greater effort of imagination to envisage them as they were in their heyday, but there are some careful full-size reconstructions. From a modeller's perspective a photographic record of parts of buildings and details such as doorways, windows, walling and groundwork will provide a store of information that can be used in future modelling projects. When a closely observed source is used as reference then a model will always carry a conviction that will be lacking in one that has simply been dreamed up. Imagination is no substitute for observation.

RECORDING INFORMATION

Most of my recording work in the field is done with a small hand-held Olympus 'mju-1' 35mm automatic camera. My SLR, with its tripod and assorted close-up rings and lenses, rarely leaves the studio. I also keep a sketchbook as a supplement to the camera, in which I use a sort of visual shorthand to record details. These rough jottings can be worked up in the studio to more finished drawings while they are still fresh in the memory. I rarely find drawing outdoors worthwhile, given the British climate, so my sketchbook is mainly an indoor tool.

CHURCH MONUMENTS

Carved military tomb effigies are to be found in a large number of churches and cathedrals throughout England, though Scotland has not been as fortunate - many of her medieval monuments fell prey to iconoclasts in the wars of religion. The knights commemorated can often be identified from the heraldry carried on their shield or surcoat. Tomb effigies provide a rich source of information for the modeller; they illustrate the development of knightly dress in fascinating detail, from the 13th century to the end of our period, and are the nearest we have to portraits of the men who fought at Bannockburn and Crécy.

Not all of these monuments are military, of course; the knights are often accompanied in their final rest by their richly attired ladies. Though the colours have long gone from the effigies the wealth of detail in the clothing and the elaborate head-dress offers a source of subject matter that has rarely been addressed by modellers.

Monuments in churches are often awkwardly positioned and may have to be

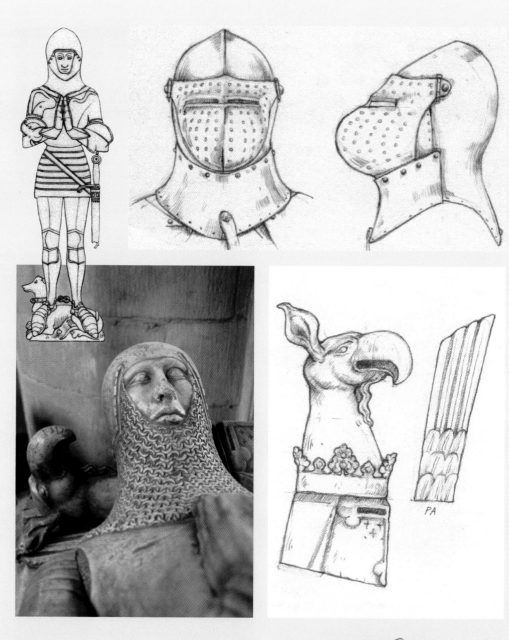

photographed in sections and supplemented by drawings to build up a complete record. There can be problems interpreting some features, and we know that sculptors sometimes omitted details - even the Black Prince's magnificent effigy in Canterbury Cathedral lacks the fastening straps on the armour. So perhaps we shouldn't be too surprised that early effigies invariably display mail-clad feet with no hint of the shoes that must have been worn beneath, or the boots that would surely have been worn on campaign in rainy Scotland.

Details of the many military effigies in England (and I doubt whether any of them have escaped being written up somewhere in some detail) can be found in the journals of various county archaeological societies in the local collections of public libraries. Nicholas Pevsner's guides to *The Buildings of England*

contain details of the various monuments to be found in each county.

We are fortunate that in addition to the many sculptured monuments there is a similar wealth of monumental brasses in our parish

FAR LEFT, TOP Drawing by the author of the monumental brass of Richard Fox at Arkesden, Essex; 1439. The armour, though as yet without tassets, is of a highly developed form and unmistakably of Italian origin. The 'great bascinet' is shown here with the visor omitted to reveal the knight's face.

TOP RIGHT The visor is included in these views of a great bascinet of similar form to that of Richard Fox. This type of helmet did not articulate as it was fastened to the shoulders, though there was room for some movement of the head inside.

FAR LEFT, CENTRE The most striking feature of the effigy of Sir Hugh Despencer in Tewkesbury Abbey is the extraordinary crest topping his helm. The grotesque griffin's head rests on stylised wings which for ease of representation have been carved out of position. They would have been fastened to the sides of the coronet.

CENTRE RIGHT Sir Hugh's head rests on his 'great helm', obscuring some of the detail, so I made a series of hasty jottings and sketches on the spot in the dimly lit abbey and relied on these to reconstruct Sir Hugh's crested helm later in the studio. I have drawn one of the wings next to the helm rather than in position, where it would have obscured much of the detail of the crest.

BOTTOM Heraldic seals, though they lack colour, serve to display coats of arms, details of armour and often heraldic crests which are not to be found elsewhere. The seal of John de St John, who fought in the Scottish Wars of Edward I, displays all these features. The seal is from the Barons' Letter to the Pope of 1300, and Sir John's winged lion crest is one of the earliest illustrations of a three-dimensional crest in medieval art (Author's drawing)

TOP RIGHT Tomb effigies of a knight and lady, later part of the 15th century. The tomb was well lit by natural light but in a cramped position that obliged me to photograph it in two halves. The very individual head of the effigy suggests that this may be a portrait of the knight. He wears a collar of S's which derives from a badge of Henry IV and attests to his Lancastrian allegiance; later effigies of adherents of the House of York have a collar of alternating suns and roses. The knight's crest, on which his head rests, is a fish, probably a 'lucy' or pike. The gothic-style armour with its rather old-fashioned gauntlets points to a date in the 1460s.

RIGHT Hans Trauner photographed the effigy of Otto von Orlamunde in the church at Himmelkron in Bavaria. The colour is probably a restoration, but provides an indication of how this wonderful polychrome monument must have looked when erected in the 1340s. The construction details of the 'coat of plates' can be seen clearly; this type of body defence was widely used in England as well, but is generally obscured on English monuments by a heraldic surcoat.

churches. The earliest of these date from around 1300 and display the finest craftsmanship; in general the quality of brasses declines towards the end of the 15th century. Monumental brasses can be found listed chronologically and illustrated in a single volume published by Her Majesty's Stationery Office (see Bibliography).

CIVIC SCULPTURE

Often underrated, the statues of famous figures of the past that furnish our urban squares and parks are worth examining. On the Continent they celebrate their heroes too; thus the imperious equestrian bronze of the Black Prince in City Square in Leeds finds a counterpart in Brittany in Dinan's heroic statue of Bertrand du Guesclin. Though both of these belong to the early years of this century (and, like most retrospective pieces, cannot necessarily be trusted as accurate reference to costume and armour), they do have an artistic value for the miniaturist. They are, essentially, finely sculpted medieval models on the grand scale, and we should take note of such work by our classically trained forebears.

OPPOSITE CENTRE Effigy of Konrad von Heideck; 14th century military equipment shared many common features throughout Europe, and there are striking similarities between the Bannockburn statue of Bruce and this effigy of c.1310 from a monastery church in Bavaria. There is no evidence of armour manufacture in medieval Scotland, and it is probable that the knightly classes in both Scotland and England imported theirs from Continental centres of production. Konrad's effigy displays an early representation of a bascinet with the camail attached by staples, similar to that employed by Pilkington Jackson to enable him to portray the Bruce's face. Note the way in which the short plate defences for the forearms fasten over an undergarment. Four chains are attached to the coat-of-plates and issue from slits in the surcoat to secure the dagger, sword and helm - but the purpose of the fourth eludes me. (Photo Hans Trauner)

FAR LEFT Jeanne d'Arc, la Pucelle, 1412-31: I chanced upon this superb over-life-size equestrian bronze some years ago during a cycling holiday in Normandy. The girlish figure contrasts sharply with the virile muscularity of her mount (though Voltaire would have it that she was 'a tavern girl of robust make'). The sculptor has dispensed with the upper part of the cuirass and introduced an erotic note by emphasising the shape of the mail-clad breasts of his 'medieval babe'. Reference to large scale sculpture such as this can help not only with the pose but with the anatomical detail of a horse; sharp-eyed readers will note the influence of the statue on the model of Robert Clifford's charger in Chapter 3. In addition, compare the fall of the folds in the Maid's flag with those in Warwick's banner in Chapter 6.

ABOVE RIGHT The modern equestrian sculpture of 'Robert the Bruce, King of Scots' was sculpted by C.Pilkington Jackson and erected on the battlefield at Bannockburn near Stirling in 1965 to mark the 650th anniversary. The Bruce's skull was discovered in Dunfermline Abbey in 1819 and casts of this were used by the sculptor to reconstruct the king's appearance. Though mail armour was still the knight's main defence at the beginning of the 14th century, by the 1330s plate had been developed as a defence for all parts of the body. It is difficult to decide exactly what stage armour development had reached at a transitional date such as 1314, and a good deal of speculation from fragmentary evidence went into the reconstruction of the Bruce's armour.

RIGHT Aymer de Valence, Earl of Pembroke, drawn after Stothard by the author. Pembroke was one of the English commanders at the battle of Bannockburn, and his tomb in Westminster Abbey was erected about 1324. This remarkably unconventional figure from the gable of his tomb displays surprisingly advanced plate armour for its time; in particular, the bascinet with moveable visor is the earliest representation of such a helmet. The Pembroke tomb supplied first hand information which helped the author to attempt his own reconstruction of Robert the Bruce at Bannockburn.

RIGHT The result of research on Iona was this 80mm model of a West Highland chief of the late 1300s. The heraldic colours remain speculative for lack of evidence. I believe that the padded fabric defence may have been weatherproofed with pitch, but I omitted this unattractive feature.

BELOW RIGHT Effigy of Bricius MacKinnon on Iona. A cold, windy, rain-lashed, day-long bike ride across the island of Mull led me to the Isle of Iona - where for the first time that summer the sun appeared, and the effigy of Bricius MacKinnon that had brought me there lived up to expectation. A number of these vigorous grave slabs of late 14th century Lords of the Isles have been collected under one roof on the island; the carvings still retain a wealth of detail, clearly illustrating the rather old fashioned military equipment of this essentially sea-borne West Highland culture. The heraldic devices on the shield include a galley with a flag, a lion, and an otter pursuing a salmon within a trefoiled double tressure. Body armour consists of a padded and vertically quilted 'akheton'; the characteristic West Highland sword with its lobated pommel is prominently displayed.

FAR RIGHT The earliest homogenous armour now to be seen in Britain - i.e., a complete harness, not retrospectively assembled from separate parts - is this North Italian example of about 1460 in the Scott Collection in Glasgow. Late 15th century armour is rare in our museums, and earlier examples are practically non-existent. The tassets are missing from the Glasgow armour, but I have restored these in my drawing and suggested an alternative form.

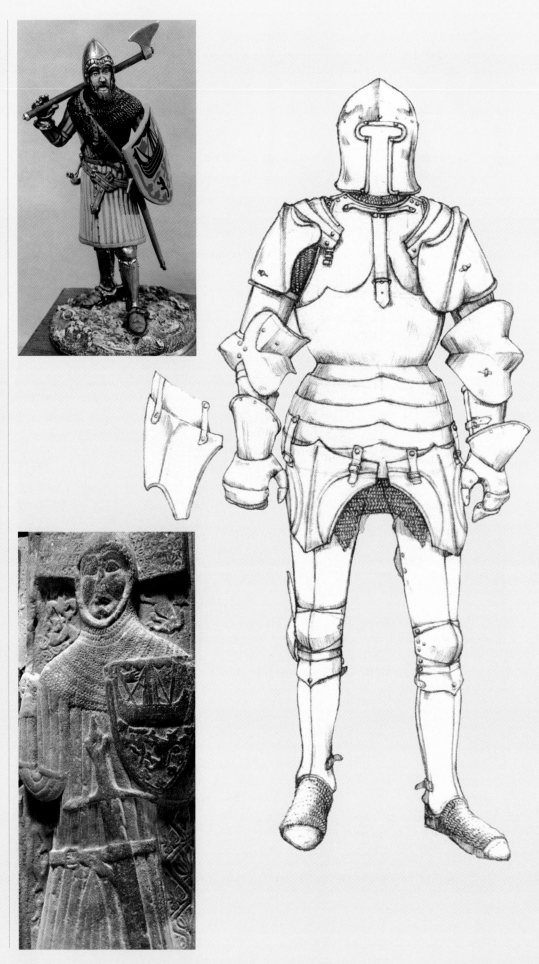

CHAPTER 2

THE SCOTTISH WARS

The modelling projects featured in Chapters 2 to 6 here progress chronologically from the early 14th century through the Hundred Years War to the time of the Wars of the Roses. My first project is a fairly simple affair, set in the time of the Scottish War of Independence which began in 1296 when Edward I of England, known as the 'Hammer of the Scots', attempted to subjugate his northern neighbour to his iron will.

The great Scottish patriot William Wallace had some success against the English, notably at Stirling Bridge in 1297; but it was only after the death of Edward I that the tide began to turn in the Scots' favour. Robert the Bruce's victory at Bannockburn in 1314 over Edward I's inept son Edward II was the high point of Scottish success. Warfare between the English and the Scots continued sporadically for many years, though the War of Independence ended in 1328 when Scotland's freedom was guaranteed – if only briefly – by the youthful Edward III of England.

THE PROJECT

I decided to model a knight from the time of the battle of Bannockburn in a simple setting, to include a few interesting battlefield accessories, and to set the figure against part of a rather forbidding Scottish castle. The knights of this time were armed in a mixture of plate and mail armour over which a surcoat was worn, so the figure presents the challenge of a variety of different textures and imposes the problem of painting some simple heraldry. I'm sure that modellers new to the period will get a good deal out of a project such as this, and more experienced modellers should be pleased with the result too. This initial project employs simple, basic techniques in the construction both of the knight himself and of the building included as a background. These techniques will be used and referred to throughout the book, and other ways of applying the basic methods – as well as more advanced techniques – will be introduced and described in later chapters.

The choice of a nominal 80mm scale affords ample scope for including all the

LEFT David de Brechin had English lands in the county of Cumberland as well as in Scotland. In 1314 he fought for Edward II at Bannockburn, where he was taken prisoner. He changed his allegiance to the Scots, but in 1320 he was implicated in a plot against King Robert and was executed at Perth.

elements of the design in a fairly restrained space. Figures standing 80mm high without their headgear are taken to represent a man about six feet tall; the scale is therefore 13mm = 1ft, or roughly 1:24. This must be borne in mind when working out, e.g., the size of a banner, the length of an arrow or sword blade, and when constructing any of the accessories or parts of buildings described.

Though it is essential that a figure's equipment and weapons are to scale and that horses are in the correct proportion to their riders, it can be permissible to use some license when creating the setting or background. In the creation of a miniature work of art correct scale is only one aspect of the process; it is a useful tool, but we need not be its slave. We shall see what this means in practical terms as the building of the model progresses.

RIGHT The first stage; the underlying plywood structure is strong and provides a solid foundation to build on. Layers of ply have been removed around the doorway, and to make a recess above it for the heraldic panel.

FAR RIGHT The building and the groundwork are taking shape simultaneously. I have started to build up the relief detail of the door surround, the steps, and the heraldic panel above. Note the method of building up the texture of the masonry in two stages of development: on the left of the wall the paper stones are glued in place; towards the right the work is more advanced, as Milliput is used to add variety.

THE DESIGN

There are probably as many ways of going about making a model as there are modellers to go about it, but the logical sequence of steps set out below is my personal way of working.

At the very outset I try to visualise the scene in my mind's eye in as much detail as possible, so really only the creative imagination is needed. It can be a help to do a thumbnail sketch simply to record these ideas; however, with a three-dimensional model it is as well to get the actual construction under way as soon as possible, and work out the design problems in the round rather than placing too much reliance on a drawing. With this point in mind I repaired to the workshop.

BASIC STRUCTURE

Too large a base with only one figure would look decidedly underpopulated, so a half-inch plywood base 6ins square was selected and sawn to size. Plywood carves easily with ordinary wood chisels, and the thin glued layers make it easy to cut the required contours. A back panel 10ins high was also cut from ply, as the thickness of the wood would be needed when a doorway was pierced through it. The wall running at right angles to the entrance can be formed from a piece of card as there are no openings in it to betray the fact. I decided that the groundwork needed to slope away from the walls in both directions,

so the outline of the door was drawn in at an appropriate height on the back panel - some steps up to it would need adding later.

The knight is equipped in the manner of the second decade of the 14th century, so though the architectural details can be earlier than this, they can't be later. Refinements in the castellated buildings of this time are unusual, especially in Scotland; however, doorways are the most likely feature to be decorated and to display evidence of when they were built, so care had to be exercised not to introduce any anachronistic details. I decided that the door should have a pointed arch since these were used in Scotland throughout the 13th century; but the size of the doorway in relation to the figure remained a problem.

For some time I'd had in my photographic collection a print of a castle doorway in Scotland that was too interesting not to use. The arch could be interpreted as a four-centered one, which would date it to the 16th century, but I thought that the true shape could safely be ignored. The main point of interest was the carving surrounding the arch, and this seemed to belong to an earlier period. It was in fact a flight of barbaric fantasy; I thought it was probably a descendant of a much earlier tradition of decoration, with its roots were in Scotland's Celtic past. Perhaps originally it had been the guardian spirit of the building, designed to overawe unwanted

FAR LEFT The carved detail above the arch and the mouldings surrounding it are at an early stage in this detail. The paper shapes which represent the ashlar blocks below the decorative knot have been carefully cut to shape; the shapes used for the random masonry are less controlled.

LEFT Note the various materials that I used to make the texture of the masonry and the surround to the heraldic panel.

ABOVE The masonry is beginning to look impressive, the heraldic panel is nearing completion, and the doorway needs a door.

visitors or ward off evil spirits? A careful assessment of the balance between artistic licence and anachronism decided me in favour of using the doorway; I'd have to make the arch a little more pointed, but I decided that it could only add to the appeal of the model.

I had made a note of the dimensions of the actual castle door on the back of the photograph, but it is really only important that the scale of the model door convinces and relates to the knight visually, for architectural features were related to the human scale in the past. The doorway was to be some distance behind the knight, far enough away that if I were to take some liberties with the scale - in effect, to shrink it somewhat - it would not be noticed. I marked on the wall what I thought was a height that would work for the door, then drew the door's centre line to fix its position.

The base was now clamped to a workbench and carved to approximately the shape required with a bevel-edged chisel; it was then offered up to the wall section, and the two were screwed together temporarily. The relationship between the knight and the door now needed to be established, so a locating hole was drilled in the base and the knight was temporarily positioned in his setting so that the composition could be assessed from a distance (the brass rods I had added to the knight's arms and legs allowed the kit to be pegged together at this stage). Several

alternative holes were drilled and the figure was variously repositioned until a satisfactory composition was arrived at; the extra holes would later disappear under the groundwork. The knight was then removed to be assembled and painted as a separate assembly.

The outline of the doorway was finished off at this stage. Half of the arch was drawn on the wood, from which a tracing was made and reversed to ensure that the arch was symmetrical. A second outline of the doorway was drawn 10mm outside the first and scored deeply with a craft knife; the layers of ply were successively removed until I had cut a 5mm recess, deep enough to build up the decorative moulding around the door. A small recess was also marked out for a heraldic panel above the entrance, then the outline was scored and a single layer of ply removed with a lino cutter.

I decided at this stage that the design of the model would be improved by adding more of the building at right angles to the doorway to give a more enclosed feel to the scene. This was formed from card; as there were to be no openings its thickness was unimportant. It was reinforced from behind with softwood, and the open score mark at the corner was filled with cocktail sticks, which would carve well when the 'stonework' was added. The workshop stage was now complete, and the more demanding detail work could begin in the comfort of the studio.

ABOVE The wooden door and its fittings are displayed here to show the construction details. The background photograph was taken at Barholm Tower in Kirkcudbrightshire, and shows the doorway that inspired the model.

ABOVE CENTRE The wooden door is in place and work is underway on the decorative hinges. The moulding of the doorway is as yet unfinished, and on the right of the picture you can see the cocktail stick formers in place.

ABOVE RIGHT The modelling work complete. When I started the doorway I didn't realise that it would ultimately prove more difficult and time-consuming than detailing and building the knight - but I derived just as much satisfaction from it as I did from the figure modelling.

DETAILING THE BUILDING

A cross-section of the moulding round the doorway was drawn, from which I was able to work out the shapes I would need to build it; not surprisingly, these turned out to be square, half-round and round. The upright section of moulding was straightforward enough. I glued a piece of 3mm square wood in the corner of the door recess, then split a cocktail stick to form a half-round section which I fixed on top of it. Another cocktail stick was used as a spacer next to this, and the moulding was completed by gluing a length of brass rod into the angle between this and the bottom of the recess.

The curved section was more of a challenge. The same sequence of building was followed, but the square shapes were built up with Milliput and the rounded sections were made from brass rod. The half-round shape was made from brass rod which was first annealed - i.e. softened by heating to a high temperature, then quenching in water - which made it easy to bend to shape round a former. It was then filed to the required profile and glued in place with super-glue. By progressing in this manner the door surround was carefully built up inside the recess. When this assembly had hardened the breaks between the carved stones were marked out and cut with a knife and files.

The outer moulding with its grotesque carved ornamentation was built up in stages using Milliput, starting with basic shapes and progressively adding refinement. The symmetry of the outer moulding had to be maintained despite the asymmetrical positioning of the reptilian torso, and this was ensured by using simple card formers to both mark out and push the moulding into position. (Modellers might find it useful when checking a construction for symmetry to hold the model up to a mirror, as the reflection points up any deficiencies alarmingly.) When the final detailing was complete the whole doorway was given a wash of dilute Milliput to unify the different materials used.

Attention was now paid to the heraldic panel above the door. Around this I glued a double surround of carefully mitred cocktail sticks, the outer of which was shaved with the grain to the necessary half-round profile. An infill of Milliput between these shapes was profiled correctly; then the panel was finished by detailing with applied paper stonework.

RANDOM STONEWORK

Apart from the ashlar door surround and the heraldic panel above, the rest of the building is constructed of unfaced random masonry set in a rough mortar, so some equivalent of this needed to be added to the model. I have always found this type of rough stonework, where no two stones are the same, simpler to model than more regularly coursed masonry. A stone-by-stone progression was used to detail the door surround with the help of

ABOVE **Stages in the assembly of bracken from an etched brass fret. An extensive range of plants and trees is available in this form, and though construction is rather slow the end result is worthwhile.**

ABOVE FAR LEFT **A protruding angle of wall has been added to the right of the doorway, and the groundwork is nearing completion.**

ABOVE CENTRE **Most of the masonry and the door mouldings have been painted with grey interior quality textured emulsion paint. This adds a unifying final layer of texture which will make the dry-brush work more effective.**

photographs of the original; this is a time-consuming process, but as the doorway is the only architectural feature here I thought it worthwhile to spend some time on it.

The bulk of the masonry needs to be represented in a more impressionistic manner. A much faster method of working was now adopted: quickly tearing and cutting 'stone' shapes from cartridge paper. These I divided into a series of heaps that approximated roughly to the various 'families' of stone shape that I noticed in the photos. Taking a section at a time and working from top to bottom, I liberally coated the walls with slightly diluted glue into which I positioned the paper shapes, corresponding with the patterns and juxtapositions suggested by my reference photos - these now became simply a starting point for improvisation rather than for a laborious copy as had been the case with the doorway. As each section of paper masonry was completed it was sealed in place with a generous application of white wood glue.

When this process was complete I added a little more variety to the stonework by making here and there some slightly thicker stones cut from different weights of paper. Milliput which was left over from other jobs was used before it hardened completely to enhance the surface texture of the walls in places, by troweling it into the stonework with the side of a scalpel and then working up textures and occasional detailed stones at strategic points.

THE WOODEN DOOR

Although many stone doorways have survived the passing centuries, the same cannot be said of the wooden doors that once guarded them; so I had to resort to some creative reconstruction in the modelling of the castle door and its fittings.

Using the doorway as a guide, the shape of the door was first drawn onto a piece of card and the position of the hinges indicated on this plan. The wooden strips that make up the door boards are part of a useful range of shapes produced in a variety of woods with model shipbuilders in mind. I cut several lengths of board from 5mm hardwood strip; then shaped the top, sanded the edges a little, and glued them directly onto the plan. The horizontal hinge straps were glued in place on the planking; the vertical strengtheners, which were cut from the ends of more of these straps, were added next along with a few extra rivets. I was fortunate to have a good supply of medieval hinges in my scrapbox - you could say that the door was as good as the scrapbox it came from. (The hinges could, of course, have been made to a simpler design from plasticard. Alternatively a pattern could have been fabricated of an even more complex design from which a mould could then be made to produce castings.)

The door handle is a reconstruction based on scant evidence so, as my scrapbox produced nothing of use this time, it was fabricated from

RIGHT Real wooden planking and miniature metal door fittings add convincing textures to the completed doorway. The ashlar mouldings and steps have been painted a warm sandstone colour to contrast with the cooler grey of the surrounding masonry.

FAR RIGHT The plan underlying the groundwork is revealed in this view from the wallhead. A distinct yet subtle diagonal movement across the foreground, punctuated only by the steps, helps lead the eye into the composition.

brass wire on a backing plate of white metal with soldered rivet detail. The metalwork of the door was finished by wire brushing, after which the relief was picked out in black and a coat of thin varnish was applied overall. Some subtle variations of colour were introduced into the woodwork by tinting the varnish with hints of enamel pigment.

GROUNDWORK

The various projects described in this book will feature a wide variety of materials and ways of producing groundwork, which we define as a small area of landscape. There are no special techniques or materials that are peculiar to particular periods of history; groundwork is universally the same. Most models, of whatever historical period, benefit from the inclusion of a certain amount of groundwork. I intend to concentrate on aspects of the subject which the reader may not come across elsewhere, and on techniques that I have evolved myself.

Large areas of groundwork need to be broken up and enlivened with incident to make them interesting, and such a problem presented itself in the area in front of my castle walls. The solution is to have some reference material available to stimulate the imagination. The photos of the actual building from which I had modelled the doorway and masonry showed only a confusion of rubble

and a tangle of undergrowth in front of the ruined tower house; so I put these aside and resorted to invention. The elements that made up the groundwork were arranged to give a diagonal feel to the composition, so that the landscape sloped away from the inner angle of the building and the rocks and grass contributed to this subtle movement. This device, which gives a little order to what could otherwise be a chaotic arrangement of shapes, can be further elaborated by the tonality employed when the landscape is painted, and by the positioning of accessories such as discarded weapons.

I keep a stock of landscaping materials in a separate work box, and this provided me with cork tile to make the rocks that form the foundation of part of the tower. In addition I used real stones from the garden, card, grass matting, and liberal quantities of Milliput and glue. I added some bracken cut from an etched brass fret to give a particularly Scottish feel to the scene, first soldering the short etched stalk to a longer rod of thin brass so that I could position the delicate plants and then remove them for painting.

PAINTING THE BUILDING & GROUNDWORK

Probably the most important stage in painting the building is the priming of the stonework with a fine textured interior masonry

LEFT The completed section of tower house. Once the camera steps back to reveal the limited extent of the model, the illusion of reality passes.

paint. This helps both to unify the different materials and to blur the edges of the paper stonework realistically. In parts two coats of primer were applied to achieve this end. A certain amount of the primer can be applied to appropriate parts of the groundwork too, as it helps to have a finely textured base when dry-brushing the colour onto the model.

Dry-brushing requires a quick-drying medium, and though I used matt enamels an equally good result can be achieved with acrylic paints. I worked with a restricted range of colours using only black, white and the primaries, which helped unify the colour scheme and simplified colour mixing. Working from dark to light, I dry-brushed the colours onto the relief in progressively lighter tones. In certain areas, such as the moulded door

surround, I finished the relief effect with a sable brush and thin colour to add outlines and highlights.

THE KNIGHT

CHOOSING THE COAT-OF-ARMS

The knight's arms would be displayed on his shield and often on his surcoat; however, evidence from contemporary sources such as monumental effigies and brasses, seals and manuscript illustrations suggests that surcoats were not uncommonly plain without any heraldic devices. The early brass of Robert de Septvans of 1306 clearly does show a heraldic surcoat, however. This displays winnowing fans, and the presence of these devices suggests that the surcoat must have been blue,

RIGHT Scottish shields and weapons are displayed against the tower walls. The shield on the left belongs to Angus Og MacDonald, who led the men of Argyll and the Isles into action at Bannockburn. In the centre is a spiked and studded Highlander's shield that might have been carried by one of Angus's men at that battle. On the right is the shield of Sir James Douglas; a heart was added to these arms in the 1330s to commemorate 'the good Sir James', who was killed in Spain while fulfilling his promise to the dying King Robert to carry his heart in battle against the Saracens. The galley on Angus's shield and the three stars of Douglas are water-slide transfers; I have never found it easy to paint a series of similar geometric shapes freehand. Painting over the transfer stars improved the effect (and disguised how I painted them so accurately...)

RIGHT Henry Percy's heraldic seal, from the Barons' Letter to the Pope of 1300. Henry purchased Alnwick Castle along with the barony from Anthony Bek, Bishop of Durham in 1309, and founded the fortunes of the Percy family, who were to become Earls of Northumberland. He fought at Bannockburn in June 1314 and his death was reported in October the same year, possibly as a result of injuries sustained in the battle. (Author's drawing)

the same colour as the background of his shield.

With regard to surcoats, there are three interesting monuments from this period in Westminster Abbey. The enamelled copper effigy of William de Valence, Earl of Pembroke has a white surcoat scattered with small shields bearing the arms of Valence. His son Aymer's tomb is here too; one of the English commanders who survived Bannockburn, he displays his arms covering the surcoat as an overall pattern. The fine stone tomb sculpture of Edmund 'Crouchback', the youngest brother of Edward I 'Longshanks', displays the arms of England with a label of France for difference on the upper part of his surcoat above the waistbelt. These examples will provide modellers with some indication of the variety of ways in which heraldry can be displayed on a surcoat. Some coats-of-arms lend themselves readily to use as an overall pattern, others are best treated otherwise. Royalty and the great lords of the land would most likely have displayed their arms on both shield and surcoat, but it is probable that many lesser knights wore a simple undecorated garment.

I decided at the outset that the model should illustrate a particular character who took part in the Scottish wars. There is a good deal of information readily available on the heraldry of these knights, providing us with a wide choice of appropriate arms. Many early 14th century coats-of-arms were very simple (the simplest of all was that of Edmund de la Brette who fought at the battle of Falkirk – his arms were simply 'gules', i.e. plain red without any heraldic devices at all). There were several Scottish coats-of-arms which recommended themselves by their simplicity and

effectiveness. Robert Bruce, later King of Scots, bore as Lord of Annandale 'Or, a saltire and chief gules'; Sir Robert Menzies bore 'Argent, a chief gules'; and Sir James Douglas's arms were 'Argent, on a chief azure three mullets argent' - these are all to be found illustrated elsewhere in this book, and readers will find some of the mysteries of heraldic terminology unravelled between Chapters 4 and 5.

The arms of many English knights are known from the heraldic seals attached to the so-called Barons' Letter to the Pope of 1300 (which has survived, as it seems fortunately not to have been sent to Rome). This is just one of several sources which provide invaluable information. The Falkirk Roll of 1298 describes the arms of 115 of the knights who fought in the battle on the English side; and the contemporary *Rime of Caerlaverock*, describing Edward I's siege of the castle in 1300, contains descriptions of the arms of over 100 of his knights. (See also under Heraldry in the Bibliography.)

I decided to paint the figure as the Scottish knight David de Brechin, whose arms are given as 'Or, three piles in point gules' in a book of Scottish armorial seals; the slightly

later Balliol Roll of 1333 contained a De Brechin - who may have been his son - and filled in more detail. The arms presented me with an attractive colour scheme and heraldry that would be simple to draw on both the surcoat and shield.

ASSEMBLY & DETAILING

The castings were first examined and any mould marks carefully cleaned off. These marks are normally scraped away easily, though when they are exaggerated into a true 'step' due to faulty mould-making they are unacceptable; they should be considered as reject castings and returned to the manufacturer. 'Stepped' mis-casting faults across plate armour are difficult to fettle, and impossible if across an area of mail.

I cut away the peg under the left foot and drilled well up into the leg with my Expo Mini-Drill. Into this I glued a length of one millimetre brass rod, to locate in a hole in the plywood base. A hole was drilled in the top of the neck and a brass rod inserted; then the helm was drilled to take this rod, to make the helm removable at this stage. I usually solder these brass pegs in place, but super-glue can

ABOVE The components of the knight are all displayed here, cleaned up and wire-brushed. The plate armour has been burnished, and brass locating rods have been soldered in place to ease assembly. Note alternative right arms with sword or axe.

inserted later, and the right foot had a rod inserted below the toes.

Roger de Trumpington's well-known memorial brass of 1298 is the only early brass to feature a helm, and it shows a retaining chain for this fixed to the waistbelt. I decided to add this feature using a piece of fine silver chain, though base metal chain of about the right scale is available. Whatever is used the chain links need to be flattened to look right, and I did this by gently squeezing each link in turn into an oval shape with a pair of jeweller's pliers. I fastened the chain to the helm with a loop of fine brass wire which was pushed into a hole drilled in the back rim of the helm; it would attach to the waist in a similar way at a later stage. Brass wire can be softened before bending by annealing it: simply heat part of the wire in the flame of a lighter until it glows cherry red, then let it cool gradually. It will then be much easier to push into shape.

I decided to continue improvements to the basic kit by changing the way that the shield is held. As readers will gather from a later paragraph, the forearm should be at an angle to the back of the shield and not horizontal to it. Changing this feature should make the pose more dynamic as well as correcting an inaccuracy. With this end in mind I removed the cast detail from the back of the shield, and cut away part of the straps cast on the knight's arm so as to improve its fit against the shield. The pad for the forearm was now remodelled in Milliput in the right position, and the shield arm was pushed into this to assure a snug fit before the straps were remodelled and the assembly put aside to cure. I decided to use an alternative arm for this kit which is available brandishing a battle axe. A sword hilt was discovered in the spares box, and this was fitted to the empty scabbard. Before beginning the assembly work I first wire-brushed the mail and then burnished and polished the plate armour.

As a good deal of time had been spent working on the castings the actual assembly of the kit was both straightforward and relatively simple. The choice of glue or solder for this job is a matter of individual preference, but I favour a mixture of low-melt solder and super-glue with the addition of a little Milliput to help out. The surcoat back and right leg was fixed in place on the main casting, then this subassembly and the other components were undercoated with thin matt white enamel. I was careful not to get paint on the burnished armour, however, as this was to be varnished. (A step-by-step account of how I burnished,

ABOVE Simple yet strikingly effective, the arms of Sir David de Brechin are painted on his shield. Work on the surcoat is at an early stage; a coat of yellow has been applied and the heraldry has been outlined in red. The same colours are echoed by the fan crest and streamers. On the right, fixed on a rod for ease of handling, is an alternative dragon crest; I thought it was a good idea when I made it, but I haven't found a use for it yet.

also be used effectively. Alternatively, if the location holes are drilled the same size as the rod, then a simple push fit will serve (the rod should be grooved down its length with a rough file before being pushed home). I inserted brass pegs into the arms and the separate leg and drilled their location holes; now the main elements of the kit could be temporarily assembled without using glue.

The breathing holes in the helm were drilled deeper by using a drill bit fixed in a pin chuck - a delicate operation best performed by rotating the pin chuck in the fingers rather than by using a power tool. The 'sights' were similarly deepened, and a hole was drilled to allow light behind the nasal bar. Tiny locating holes were drilled in the knight's heels for the delicate rowel spur castings which would be soldered and painted the knight, apart from being tedious, would merely repeat my comments on these techniques in Chapter 1.)

Although a history of the development of medieval armour has no place in these pages (but see Bibliography), a few comments will be of assistance to modellers interested in conversion work and in adding authentic detail. Our knowledge of armour in Europe at the time of the Scottish War of Independence is derived entirely from documentary sources, seals, monuments and manuscript illustrations, all of which present us with problems of interpretation. There is scant archaeological evidence of early medieval armour, and nothing from this time has yet come to light (apart from several swords, which attest by their fine craftsmanship to the skills of early armourers). It is not until the later part of the 14th century that archaeological finds - along with a very few pieces which have survived above ground - begin to appear. The knight of 1300 was still essentially the mailed warrior of preceding centuries, displaying very little plate armour other than the helm, though there does seem to have been a hard body defence of some kind beneath the surcoat.

The armour of the noble and knightly classes in Scotland is known only from contemporary seals and a few fragmentary surviving monuments. It was no different from that of the English knights whom they fought against, and it is probably correct to say that all the Scots knights' armour was imported from the Continent.

Most Scots, however, were neither nobility nor knights; theywould have fought on foot, and a glimpse of these early infantrymen is afforded by Robert the Bruce's parliament held at Scone in 1318, which outlined their equipment. Men worth £10 in goods were to have a sword, spear, plate gloves, and an iron hat or bascinet; their armour was to be either a padded and quilted 'akheton', or a mail shirt or 'haubergeon'. Men worth goods to the value of a cow were to be armed with a spear or bow; no armour is mentioned, although this equipment was the minimum they were required to bring on campaign. It is evident from this that a good deal of imaginative reconstruction work would have to go into creating a model of one of the men who fought alongside Wallace or Bruce. It is arguable, however, particularly in the case of the

Lowlanders who formed the bulk of Scots armies, that he may not have looked very different from his English counterpart.

(The dress of the Highland element of these armies remains highly speculative; there is practically no contemporary evidence, and we don't even know whether some form of kilt or plaid was worn at this time. Froissart, who seems for once to have been lost for words, described the appearance of Highlanders as simply 'outrageous'. We do know that the wild Celts of Galloway, doubtless fortified against the English bowmen with a copious intake of liquor, fought 'naked' in the front ranks at the Battle of the Standard outside Northallerton in 1138; I think that this probably means that they fought unarmoured rather than unclothed.)

ABOVE The heraldic surcoat is shown painted before the final assembly stage.

ABOVE LEFT AND RIGHT **Two** views of the completed model. They demonstrate the essential appeal of medieval figures in this kind of background: the grim stonework sets off the gleam of steel and the splash of sumptuous heraldic colour.

SHIELDS

Shields are one of the items that present problems to the modeller; in particular, the appearance of the back can be difficult to reconstruct. The few medieval shields that have survived are made of layers of thin, close-grained wood glued together in the manner of modern plywood. An outer facing of canvas or parchment is glued over this, and sometimes given a coat of gesso to prepare the surface for painting. On some shields the heraldry was modelled in low relief, though this technique was probably seldom seen on shields of war.

The back of the shield was covered with a fabric lining and coloured; for instance, the back of the Black Prince's funerary shield in Canterbury Cathedral is painted blue. A pad for the forearm was set at an angle behind the shield, and straps or 'enarmes' were provided, one each for the forearm and wrist and a third for the fingers if they were not holding the horse's reins. In addition a buckled and decorated 'guige' round the knight's neck helped to support the weight of the shield. The rivets by which the straps were attached passed through the shield and were hidden when the facing was added.

A fine early 14th century stone effigy at Goldsborough in Yorkshire reveals some interesting details of the back of the shield. In this case the top half carries a padded lining, thicker at the top where it would be held against the upper arm and tapering to waist level. The lining appears to be of thick leather and is nailed to the back of the shield with domed studs resembling upholstery nails. Awareness of these internal features will help modellers to add convincing detail, particularly those who like to show battle damage to their knights' shields.

CRESTS & HELMS

Some of the earliest heraldic crests can be seen on the seals attached to the Barons' Letter of 1300. Crests are unlikely to have been common on the battlefield; yet there is an instance, related by Guillaume le Breton, of Renaud Count of Boulogne creating a sensation by

LEFT Two ways of arranging the padding behind the shield are shown here, both based on monumental evidence. The arm is in a diagonal position behind the shield, which could be used to deliver an uppercut to an opponent in combat.

wearing a whalebone crest in the form of a pair of antlers at the battle of Bouvines in 1214. That both the crest and its sensational effect were specifically described perhaps points to the probability that they were highly uncommon.

Nevertheless, for the modeller the temptation to add a crest to a plain helm is sometimes difficult to resist. The most common form of crest to be seen on the Barons' seals is the so-called fan plume. It remains uncertain what material this was made from - perhaps parchment or hardened leather (cuir-bouilli) - so its recreation in miniature form is speculative. The seals obviously give no clue as to colour; but it seems certain that these crests, being items of flamboyant display, were indeed coloured, and the segmented outline suggests that they may have been painted in alternating colours. Several crests in the form of wyverns appear on the seals, along with an eagle, and a lion standing between a pair of vertical wings. In addition many of the seals show some form of scarf flying from the helmet; this may have developed from a lady's favour.

I have been asked at times by modellers who wanted to depict a knight without his helm exactly what was worn beneath it. Until the early 14th century a mail hood or 'coif' was worn under the helm, and beneath this a padded 'arming cap'. The helm had its own padded lining consisting of a headband with a series of segmented supporting straps, adjustable at the crown, by which the helm was supported on the knight's head and held firm by a chinstrap. These details are strikingly similar to the system used inside a 20th century steel helmet, and sculptural evidence confirms this. Many tomb monuments employ the device of supporting the knight's head on a crested helm laid on its side; in many cases this put the sculptor to the trouble of carving the inside of the helm and its supporting straps. A second form of arming cap had a protruding circlet of padding above the brow, presumably intended to support the helm.

MODELLING A SIMPLE FAN CREST

I began by making a full size outline drawing from measurements of the miniature helm. Then, using illustrations of the Barons' seals as a guide, I drew on a fan crest and adjusted it until I arrived at the right size. The nine segments of the fan were drawn with a protractor and extended beyond the semicircle of the crest, which turned out to be about the same diameter as a 5 pence coin. I rolled out a small amount of Milliput and put it aside to harden. Later in the modelling session, when the Milliput was about leather hard, I used the coin as a template to cut out a semicircle, and mounted it on a brass rod. This was fixed over the drawing with masking tape, and the segments were drawn on with the help of the extended lines. It is difficult to decide what the segments are; do the lines represent incised or raised divisions, or do they indicate a colour change?

When faced with a dilemma like this I always work on the part of a project that I

ABOVE Battle damage: the shield of the Scots knight Sir Robert Menzies displays the plywood construction method beneath the damaged outer facing.

RIGHT The fan crest can be seen cut to shape on the scale working drawing which was also used to mark out the coloured segments. On the right the painted crest is mounted on the helm by means of a brass rod. The lower drawing of a seal from the Barons' Letter shows the source I used for the crest and streamers.

understand and leave what I don't understand until later, hoping that with luck the problem will take care of itself. With this axiom in mind, I carved the edge of the crest to shape, rounded off the top, and made a shallow file cut to indicate the segments which would later be further emphasised by painting them alternate colours. The knight's helm was drilled to take the brass locating rod of the crest; and the scarf which appears prominently flying from many of the barons' helms was now considered. There were two styles of these: one was an informal looking attachment in the shape of a lady's headscarf, the other a more formal streamer which I thought looked well with the fan crest. The streamer could have been made from Milliput, but I chose metal foil as being more malleable allowing me to bend and adjust the streamer when it was attached to the helm.

AILETTES

These curious appendages were much in vogue at the time of our model; they have at times been variously misinterpreted by modellers and illustrators, and their purpose has been the subject of debate. Ailettes or 'little wings' are usually depicted on monumental brasses at right angles to their true situation on the shoulders in order for the viewer to see them from the front. They were in fact laced to the points of the shoulders to be seen from the side; they were purely decorative, and their purpose was the display of heraldry - they had no defensive function. The latest brass in this country to include them is that of Sir John de Bacon at Gorelston in Suffolk, who died in 1321. In that case the ailettes, which one would expect to display his personal arms, are charged with those of St George of England; Argent, a cross gules.

LEFT Sir John de Clavering displays his arms on his surcoat, shield, ailettes and lance pennon; his red and gold crest reflects the colours of the heraldry. The paternal arms of Clavering are 'Quarterley or and gules, a riband sable'; these were differenced by Sir John in his father's lifetime by a 'label azure' - the colour of the label seems to be an arbitary choice or may be due to artistic taste rather than being dictated by any system at this time. Both father and son fought at the battle of Falkirk in 1298; Sir John was taken prisoner at Bannockburn in 1314 and later released on payment of a large ransom.

SCOTLAND'S HEROES
WILLIAM WALLACE & ROBERT THE BRUCE

RIGHT Helm and crest of the King of Scots from the Armorial de Gelre. (Author's drawing)

Scotland's national hero, William Wallace, has proved elusive to illustrate convincingly, and he remains a challenge to which modellers have as yet proved unequal. He was not of the knightly classes, and it is inappropriate to depict him as the chivalric hero knight. The well-known statue of Wallace as Guardian of Scotland erected in 1888 in Aberdeen nevertheless immortalises him in heroic pose as a 13th century knight. (Nor was Wallace a hairy bushranger with funny warpaint and late 20th century political views - a role in which he has lately been portrayed in a juvenile distortion of history which crossed the threshold into the realm of fantasy.)

Despite his fame Wallace remains a shadowy historical figure. We know nothing of his early life, though the recent rediscovery of the seal he used as Guardian of Scotland after the battle of Stirling Bridge in 1297 seems to confirm his origins in Ayrshire in south-west Scotland. Wallace is generally - if somewhat speculatively - credited with the arms 'Gules, a lion rampant argent'; this is sometimes shown with a blue and white border, presumably to signify that his father was still alive - however, this is an anachronism, as no such heraldic difference existed in Wallace's time.

RIGHT Displayed against the wall of a tower are the shields of the Earl of Carrick and his elder brother Robert the Bruce, Lord of Annandale. On the right the shield bearing 'Argent, a lion rampant azure' has been attributed to Robert the Bruce as head of that house. Since completing this model I have discovered in the course of research that there is no evidence that the Bruce ever displayed these arms, neither is there any reason to believe that Edward Bruce bore them differenced by a crescent argent. These are the arms of the Yorkshire Bruces, and are the source of some confusion.

RIGHT Arms and crest of the Lord of Annandale from the Armorial de Gelre. (Author's drawing)

LEFT The Bruce was considered to be 'one of the three most accomplished knights in Christendom' in his day. Adrian Bay modelled this grimly purposeful 'Bruce at Bannockburn'; astonishingly, the model is a conversion of the Border Miniatures 80mm mounted kit of the same subject pictured above. Note the convincing treatment of the muddied edge of the caparison, and a couple of its appliquéd escutcheons starting to come unstitched. (Photo A.Bay)

ABOVE 'King Robert the Bruce at Bannockburn, 1314', painted by the author from one of his own Border Miniatures kits.

(i)

(ii)

King Robert has proved a more fruitful subject and several well-known modellers have produced fine models of The Bruce. He is depicted on his Great Seal of 1316 with a crowned helm and bearing the Royal Arms of Scotland on his shield, surcoat and horse trapper. The Armorial de Gelre compiled later in the 14th century illustrates the helm and crest of the King of Scots. The helm is crowned and crested by a red lion seated and brandishing a sword; the mantling bears the arms of The Bruce's Lordship of Annandale, 'Or, a saltire and chief gules'. These arms are to be found on the heraldic seals of the Bruces of Annandale and were the personal arms used by Robert the Bruce. The Gelre armorial shows the crest of the Lord of Annandale as a red sleeved arm topped by a gesturing hand.

Robert's brother, the brave and impetuous Edward Bruce, Lord of Galloway would have borne the arms of this lordship - 'Azure, a lion rampant argent crowned or'. In 1313 he became Earl of Carrick, so at that time he may have borne 'Argent, a chevron gules'. In 1318, as King of Ireland, he was killed in battle at Fochart near Dundalk. He may have contrived an appropriate coat of arms as king of that country, but no report of it has come down to us.

FAR LEFT 'Mayhem in the Highlands': an earlier and lesser-known Scottish hero is celebrated in this battle piece by the Lanarkshire modeller Robert Bryce. The details of this ill-documented encounter are scant, and one senses that legend has somewhat encroached on historical fact in this lively scene. The fight was between a marauding Danish war band and Scots under the Earl of Sutherland, and probably took place in the mid-13th century. The Danes were routed by the battling earl, who slew their leader in single combat - wielding the severed leg of a horse! The size of the figures diminishes from 120mm to 25mm to increase the illusion of depth in the diorama. There are 80mm figures in the middle distance, and in the background a diminutive 25mm Scots army pursues the defeated Danes.

ABOVE RIGHT The Earl of Sutherland, complete with his gory weapon. He started life as a 120mm Verlinden kit, which was cut up and repositioned, then remodelled with epoxy putty. Apparently the town of Dornoch, where this diorama is on display, has a horseshoe on its coat of arms to commemorate this deed. (Photos R.Bryce of 'Merlindale')

ABOVE Bryce's grizzled Danish leader was modelled using a nude Academy torso and a pair of Verlinden hands as a starting point. The arms, legs, head, cloak and shield were modelled from putty, plasticard, paper, metal foil and brass.

ABOVE The Scots modeller Nigel Kelman scratch-built this imposing 80mm 'Robert the Bruce'. The hollow helm was made from thin sheet metal and the finely rendered ring mail was fashioned from very fine coiled wire. (Photo N.Kelman)

THE MILITARY ORDERS
TEMPLARS & HOSPITALLERS

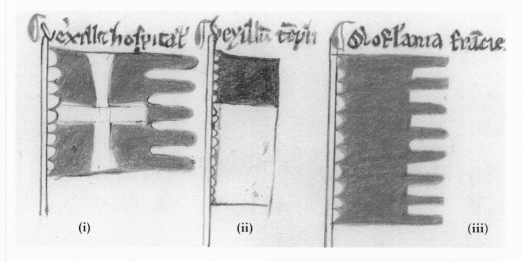

(i)   (ii)   (iii)

RIGHT I drew these banners after Matthew Paris, who drew the originals between 1244 and 1259.
(i) *Vexillum Hospitalis* - the banner of the Hospital. Matthew draws a 'cross formy', but in another version he drew a 'plain cross'. It seems likely that in the 13th century the two types of cross were interchangeable.
(ii) *Vexillum Templi* - the banner of the Temple. This was known as 'Beauséant' from the old French term *baucent* applied to piebald horses. The arms of the Temple were 'Argent, a cross gules'; this was a 'plain cross', not a 'cross patonce' as is sometimes drawn. Evidence concerning the early heraldry of the Temple and Hospital is sparse and there is much uncertainty. Recently a friend sent me an interesting set of French picture cards which illustrated the arms of all 24 Grand Masters of the Order of the Temple (see Bibliography). The last Master of the Templars in England was William de la More. He was arrested in 1308 when the Templars' lands were confiscated, but was released and given a government pension.
(iii) I drew the third banner in the group out of interest, although it is not a flag of the Military Orders. The legend above the original reads *'Oloflamma Francie'*; this is one of the earliest representations of the ancient banner of France, the 'Oriflamme'.

ABOVE RIGHT 'Last of the Hospitallers', a model by Adrian Bay from a 54mm Pegaso kit with some conversion work. Despite heroic resistance by the Military Orders, Jerusalem fell in 1243 and by the end of the 13th century the Holy Land was lost.
(Photo A. Bay)

The Knights of the Temple and of the Hospital of St John of Jerusalem were formed in the early 12th century after the establishment of the Crusader kingdoms in the Holy Land. From the outset the Templars, who were known originally as the Poor Knights of Christ, were organised as warrior monks. The Order of the Hospital was founded to care for pilgrims to the Holy Land, their role extending some years later into the military sphere via escort duties.

The last decade of the 13th century saw the collapse of the Crusader states; yet though displaced and diminished in numbers and power, the Hospitallers survived as a military organisation facing the advance of Islam, based at first on the island of Rhodes and finally on Malta. The Templars' great wealth and their activities as bankers and moneylenders aroused the enmity of King Philip of France. In 1307, amid accusations of vice, corruption and heresy, Philip had the French Templars arrested and the Pope ordered their detention throughout Europe. In France the brutal suppression of the order culminated in 1314 when 45 Templars including the Grand Master, Jacques de Molay, were burnt at the stake in front of Notre Dame.

In 1259 a Papal bull of Alexander IV ordered that the Knights of the Hospital should wear black mantles to distinguish themselves from the other brethren of the Order. In time of war and in battle they were to wear red surcoats having sewn upon them a white cross exactly as upon the banner.

LEFT 'Brian de Jay, Master of the Templars in England, 1298': model by the author, from an 80mm Border Miniatures kit. Brother Brian was killed at the battle of Falkirk in that year; by an odd coincidence so was Brother John de Sautrey, the Master of the Scottish Templars - they were practically the only casualties of note. Not long after I painted this model I read G.Brault's book *Early Blason*, which convinced me that I should have painted Brother Brian's arms as 'Argent, a cross passant gules, a chief sable'. A cross passant is a plain cross; the style I painted is a cross patonce.

BELOW Arms of the Temple:
(iv) Argent, a cross passant gules
(v) Argent, a cross passant gules, a chief sable; from Walford's Roll of Arms of 1275. (Author's drawing)

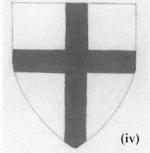

(iv)

(v)

CHAPTER 3

THE MOUNTED MEDIEVAL KNIGHT

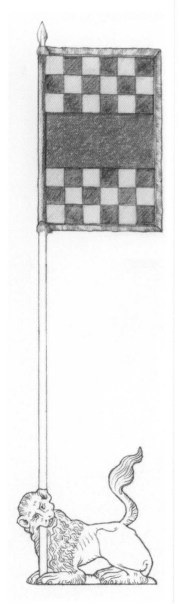

OPPOSITE Sir Robert Clifford, who fell at Bannockburn in 1314 'at the height of his martial prowess and fame'.

BELOW Banner of Robert Clifford: 'Checky or and azure, a fess gules'. (Author's drawing)

The model will take as its starting point an assemblage of commercially available castings - not quite a kit - which will be adapted to suit my purpose. This will entail a certain amount of detailing similar to that described in the last chapter, which will lead on to the next logical step of some simple conversion work. This will enable me to dictate the pose of the figure rather than having to accept that of the commercial casting. I intend to model a portrait of my subject bareheaded, so the head will need some careful thought and handling.

THE PROJECT

The particular subject that I have chosen to illustrate is Sir Robert Clifford, the castellan of Appleby in Westmorland, who, with his retinue of northern knights, fought at the battle of Bannockburn in 1314. He was one of the most notable of those killed in the two days of fighting; aged 40 at this time, and experienced in many campaigns against the Scots, he was at the height of his martial prowess and fame when he fell.

CLIFFORD'S CHARGER

Sir Robert Clifford's charger or 'destrier' was a strong, proud beast of high breeding, much like a modern heavy hunter. Medieval warhorses were not the lumbering cold-blooded giants we know as 'shire horses' today; these are agricultural beasts and were never the mounts of knights or men-at-arms. Though we don't know anything about Clifford's mount at Bannockburn we do know that he had a taste for greys, as he rode a fine dapple-grey charger valued at £30 at the battle of Falkirk in 1298. Fighting men of those days rode stallions in battle, or so the Bayeux Tapestry's embroiderers would have us believe - all the knights' horses are carefully illustrated as 'entire', not geldings. Clifford himself, at least in his youth, may have been a rather romantic figure; the poet who saw him at the siege of Caerlaverock in 1300 says of him 'If I were a young maiden I would give him my heart and person, so great is his fame'.

We know then the colour and type of horse that Clifford would probably have ridden at Bannockburn, and we know that his coat-of-arms was 'Checky or and azure, a fess gules'. The figure is to be bareheaded, and I thought that a heroic pose might be appropriate.In addition Clifford needs to be depicted armoured in the manner of the period. With these points in mind I collected together a set of castings that would give me the best possible start, needing the least conversion work. In essence I intended to mount an early 14th century knight from one mounted kit on a horse from a second kit.

The horse I chose was originally based on the mount of a rather heroic Joan of Arc that I came across in Compiègne while cycling across northern France. I thought that the romantic posture of the horse would suit the pose of the rider, and that the two would complement each other. On a practical note: I'm sure that there are many manufacturers who would not be too put out by a request to supply a different horse with a kit. It may be possible with some manufacturers' kits to mix and match horse halves and heads in a similar manner to the Historex system, but as larger scale metal kits are not really designed with this in mind it is probably more trouble than it is worth to attempt it. I planned to use compatible body halves from the same kit and to substitute a different head and tail to achieve the effect I had in mind.

ASSEMBLING THE HORSE

Though there is nothing that makes the assembly of a medieval horse different to that of any other period, I hope that readers will be interested enough in my particular methods to bear a certain amount of detail in the description.

The cast-on saddle and leather trappings in this case had a look of the late 15th century, so I decided that much of this would have to be removed and remodelled in an earlier, more appropriate style.This unwanted detail was cut away using a lino cutter with great care - always pushing it away from the fingers; then the rough surface left by this process was trimmed and scraped

smooth with a scalpel. Any awkward depressions in the casting were cleaned up in a similar manner using a curved blade; then the surface was finished with a file. Inevitably there were still rough spots where the lino cutter had dug too deep, but these were easily filled with epoxy putty and smoothed over to leave the components of the horse ready for assembly.

The two legs of the horse that contact the ground were drilled as far up into the leg as possible to take brass supporting rods. These rods were bent to ensure that they protruded from the legs vertically, then soldered into their locating holes. I prefer to use solder to assemble metal parts, as discussed in Chapter 1, but in all cases super-glue can be used as an alternative. I soldered the horse's head to the right hand body half first, from the inside so as to leave a minimum of cleaning up around the joint. I then offered the other horse half up to this. The fit of the horse halves was good and these were simple to solder together, along with the tail, though because the head was from a different kit there was a good deal of filling needed where the neck joined the body. The brass locating rods were now inserted into holes drilled in a temporary plywood base, enabling the horse assembly to stand unsupported.

ABOVE The parts I started with are displayed here; they are from my own Border Miniatures 80mm range of mounted figures. At the top is the the left hand horse half with the cast-on detail which I later removed. The bottom assembly shows this process complete, and the head soldered in place.

RIGHT The basic shapes of the saddle and trappings have been established in Milliput. They are simple yet robust, with little decoration.

The rider's surcoat covers most of the saddle, leaving only the pommel and cantle needing detailed treatment. There exist a good many contemporary representations of the type of saddle that may have been in use at Bannockburn. It is not easy to interpret these early sources with any certainty; however, they are the only reliable guide we have, and along with what we know about medieval saddles in general they should allow a convincing reconstruction.

The underlying wooden framework of a medieval saddle was called the 'tree' and consisted of four parts. The two boards which sit either side of the horse's backbone and take the rider's weight are joined together by the arches of the 'bur-plate' or pommel in front and the cantle behind. The seat fitted above the boards and between the arched pieces, and was well clear of the horse's spine. The saddle tree was padded and covered on the inside with sheepskin and on the outside with leather. The girth and fittings for the stirrup leathers were fastened to the boards. (Though I have based this description on the surviving early 15th century saddle of Henry V in Westminster Abbey, the same general principles not only apply to saddles of the preceding century, but are true of saddles in use in the Napoleonic Wars some 500 years later.) The breast band with its pendant enamelled shields was taken from a late 13th century manuscript illustration; the crupper along with its decoration was the result of suggestions from a variety of references.

ABOVE At an early stage of construction I ensured that the horse and rider would work together as a unit, with Clifford well seated in the saddle. You can see the cleaning-up process nearing completion, thought there is still work to be done on the soldered neck joint.

LEFT The saddle and crupper completed.

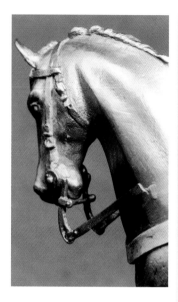

ABOVE The bit and reins are seen assembled. A short brass rod soldered in place forms a cross-brace which adds stability to this delicate assembly.

RIGHT The reins are complete in this view, and where it is practical they are fastened to the horse's neck to make a stable structure. Note also the decorative pendant shields.

THE REINS & BIT

The reins always present difficulties but they are worth spending time fiddling with. There are other ways of dealing with these, but the method I used gives a robust construction that will withstand a certain amount of handling during painting. The ends of the reins were fixed to the shanks of the bit before these were fastened in place. I made sure that the shanks lined up together, then secured a brass spacer rod between them which would help strengthen this rather delicate assembly. The reins were then led up towards the position of the rider's hand and bent to shape; where they came into contact with the horse's neck they were firmly fixed to this. The ends of the reins were fastened together and positioned so that with the rider in place his left gauntlet would slip into place over them; a loop of rein slotted into the top of the gauntlet completes the assembly. The reins were always held in this manner by riders of all nations at all times. Cast metal reins can sometimes appear rather thick but this can be remedied by trimming the visible top edge to a finer profile.

EARLY 14TH C HORSE ARMOUR

I have always considered that a high-ranking knight such as Robert Clifford, who could afford to arm himself in the best equipment of his time, would have provided his expensive and vulnerable charger with a degree of protection too. Horse-armour at the time of Bannockburn presents us with another problem: there is evidence that such armour was in use, but we have no real idea what form it took. There are puzzling references to 'barded' horses in contemporary documents which suggest some sort of protective covering. This may have been in the form of soft armour of similar construction to the padded 'gambeson' that was worn beneath the knight's mail. Complete trappers of mail have been suggested, reaching down to the horse's knees, but I think that these would not only have been impossibly heavy but would have unbalanced the horse at any gait faster than a walk. I decided that I had to leave Clifford's horse unarmoured; it is pointless to attempt an historical reconstruction when you have nothing whatever to go on.

MODELLING & DETAILING THE BASE

I used the cast metal base supplied with the horse, with the detail cut away, as the underlying structure on which to build up the groundwork. The horse has only two legs in contact with the ground and these need to be securely fixed to the base. Using the metal base meant that I was able to solder the hooves to this as well as glueing the brass supporting rods into the wood below. The weight of the horse and rider all bear on these joints and depend on their solidity for stability; a weak joint could result in the delicately balanced model keeling over. Misalignments between the holes in the base and the pegs in the hooves can happen during the casting process despite the patterns and moulds being accurate; in this case simply bend the legs back to their proper position.

I bought a low plinth of nicely figured English yew on which to mount the model eventually, and to ensure that this stayed in pristine condition I built the groundwork up on a card base rather than directly onto the polished wood. First I cut a piece of card to the same size as the working area of the plinth, and then glued the metal base to this. The card would provide support as I built up Milliput over and around the metal to form a rectangle of rough groundwork; the card would be

LEFT The modelling work on Robert Clifford's charger is complete, and the locator pins in his hooves are offered up to the holes drilled in the groundwork.

peeled off and discarded when the work was finished.

I found a targe and spear, a hunting horn and a Scottish style sword in my spares box; these would bring the base to life, and I carefully positioned them on the ground to help lead the eye inwards. The battlefield debris visually broke up the area of the base, and each of the items was now treated as a separate still-life and modelled into the groundwork. More detail was then added to give a roughly diagonal feel to the base which would help to unify the composition. A small section of metal base had been left uncovered by Milliput so that the completed horse assembly could be soldered solidly into place. With this done the groundwork round the hooves was built up, and the completed horse and base subassembly could be undercoated and put aside ready for painting.

BELOW The groundwork at an early stage, showing how Milliput is modelled over the cast metal base; some areas of grass will be added later. Here I am trying out positions for the Scottish battlefield debris.

CONVERTING & ASSEMBLING THE KNIGHT

The kit which provided my starting point for the portrait of Robert Clifford needed only simple modifications to achieve a radically different appearance. A portrait demanded a convincing head, however, and after a good deal of rummaging my spares box yielded up one that was near to what I envisaged. The body casting had a separate helmet, so it was a simple matter to hollow out the neck a little and then drill a locating hole to temporarily position the head, which was mounted on a brass rod. The helmet was put aside - this would be fastened to the rear of Clifford's saddle at a later stage.

The arms were similarly given brass locating rods, an arrangement which allowed the exact position of the head and arms to be decided on with the model in a dry state before being permanently fixed. The right arm was straightened by making a saw cut into the mail sleeve and then prising the lower arm carefully into the new position; this left the arm in a fragile state, which I stabilised with a blob of solder inside the elbow. The mail sleeve was then made good with Milliput and a mail-making tool (see Chapter 1).

As the brass mounting rod allowed the head to pivot freely I decided by trial and error on the best position for Clifford's head - looking to his left provided a nice counterpoint to the horse, which was inclining its head to the right. A mail hood, thrown back on the shoulders, was added at this stage; the basic shape was modelled in Milliput and the mail texture was added as the putty dried. At the same time I added a moustache to give some gravity to the imperious Clifford's countenance.

As a device to add more interest to the right hand side of the figure I decided to add a dagger, despite the rather slim evidence for these being carried at this time (see my remarks on Church Monuments in Chapter 1). An axe was also fixed so that it appeared to be tied to the right side of the saddle; it would provide a visual balance to the helm, which was to be slung on the other side behind the cantle. The position of the helm meant that it would need to be hollow to be effective (see Chapter 4 for a successful method of hollowing a helmet).

I turned my attention to the shield next; as Clifford's shield is slung on his back some repositioning and bending of the lower part of the guige was needed so that the end curled over the cantle to meet the bottom of the shield. I added a short length of guige to the top edge of the shield, to engage into a slot under the mail hood. A brass rod was then soldered in place on the back of the shield and a locating hole drilled in the figure, so that the shield subassembly could be positioned and then removed for painting.

STIRRUPS & SPURS

I always drill the rider's heels to take the spurs at an early stage in assembly, but add them to the model after it is assembled and painted – they are delicate and vulnerable. Medieval stirrups were fastened to the side boards of the saddle tree rather towards the front; however, in model form they are added to the rider's legs at the assembly stage, allowing him to be removed from the horse with them in place.

There is a good deal of handling and fiddling required to get the stirrups positioned convincingly, so it is best to get them right before any paint is applied. The bottom of the stirrup iron is first solidly fastened to the sole of the rider's shoe. The stirrup leather is twisted and bent into place, then soldered to the inside of the knee. The join – which can be made with liberal amounts of solder or glue, since it will be out of sight – is then trimmed with knife and file to enable the rider to slip snugly into the saddle.

ABOVE LEFT The portrait head of Robert Clifford is in place, with the moustache and mail hood modelled in Milliput.

ABOVE The right arm has been sawn three-quarters through, then bent to shape and soldered in its new position. It awaits its Milliput filling, which must be textured to match the cast mail pattern.

LEFT The feet were always thrust into the stirrups from the outside, so take care to twist the stirrup-leathers the right way.

ABOVE The modelling stage is complete; the armour has been buffed, the unarmoured areas are undercoated, and grass has been added to the base.

RIGHT I take comfort from the belief that in the early 14th century a servant in a castle in Westmorland might not have painted the 'checky' pattern of Robert Clifford's arms with mathematical perfection. The groundwork, targe and scattered weapons were all dry-brushed with the same earth colours to produce a unified effect. Only a few accents of colour and varnish were later added to highlight these.

PAINTING & FINAL ASSEMBLY

The final stages of assembly were made simple by the brass rods fitted to the arms and shield, which located them accurately in place. These parts were still separate and would only be fixed in place at the last minute after the figure was painted.

The simple geometry of Robert Clifford's coat-of-arms proved to be far from simple to paint. It would have been far quicker and much easier to paint an animate charge such as a lion rampant. Essentially the alternating checked pattern had to be six squares across, starting yellow and ending blue. The squares needed to be the same size but did not need to be painted with absolute mathematical precision; they simply needed to be neatly done. I started work on the shield first and, drawing with thin paint, I divided the top of this into six equal parts which established the size of the squares. There was then room for two rows of squares above the fess and three below, which I drew with thin enamel. This arrangement of the heraldry produced a bold and satisfying design which suited the shape of the shield well. The drawing was then filled in and the shapes refined several times using quite thin paint, until the squares were accurate and the colour opaque.

The heraldry was drawn on the surcoat in a similar manner, though in this case I drew three rows of squares first so that the fess was

LEFT I painted Clifford's arms and those of some of his northern neighbours on the pendant enamelled shields. From the centre they are: Clifford, the Temple, Latimer, Clavering and Neville.

BELOW The model is mounted on a well-proportioned base of fine English yew.

not placed too high. The checked pattern was not easy to paint on the folds in the skirts of the surcoat. I started with the relatively flat sections where it was readily apparent how the pattern should be painted, then finished the more problematic areas by a process of trial and error.

At first I considered painting Clifford's swordbelt and the horse's saddlery as faded crimson leather. This would probably have worked well, but I thought that simple brown leather saddlery made a striking enough tonal contrast with the white horse, and there was no need to introduce another colour into the scheme.

CHAPTER 4
THE HUNDRED YEARS WAR

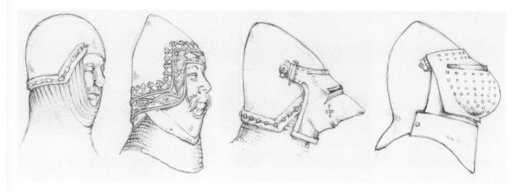

THE PROJECT

This chapter takes us into the period which cannot fail to fire the imagination of the English medieval enthusiast: the intermittent conflict between England and France which spanned the years from 1337 to 1453, and which saw some of the most legendary feats of arms in the whole of English history.

I decided to model a two-figure vignette on a square base, depicting the noted Cheshire knight Sir Robert Knollys along with an archer of his company. When I originally sculpted the archer and knight they were not designed as a pair, but I thought that if they were positioned with some thought they would interact and complement each other quite successfully. The restful pose of the middle-aged mercenary captain would contrast with the more dynamic turning posture of the archer.

SIR ROBERT KNOLLYS

Robert Knollys rose from humble beginnings to be one of the most famous and successful commanders of his time. It is probable that his military career began as a simple archer; yet he rose to such prominence that he was described by Froissart as being the most able and skilful man-at-arms in all the Free Companies. He served with distinction under the Black Prince, and amassed a very sizeable fortune in the course of the French wars. Knollys - referred to by many of his contemporaries as 'The Old Brigand' - died in comfortable retirement in about 1407. As a young man he is first mentioned in 1347 at the siege of La Roche Derien in Brittany; in 1351, as a knight,

he fought in the 'Combat of the Thirty' where he was captured. From this we can deduce that he must have lived to be about 80 years old.

The 80mm kit which I selected needed only a little simple conversion work to turn the knight into a portrait of Sir Robert in the late 1360s, when he was about 40 years of age. The style of armour was appropriate for this date, but I thought that as he appears to have just taken his helmet off an arming cap could be modelled, which would make an interesting conversion project. The knight portrayed by the kit was by no means in the first flush of youth, and the arming cap would disguise his baldness and enable me to depict a rather younger man of roughly the right age for the subject.

Sir Robert's crest was a ram's head, which bears no relation to his arms which were 'Gules, on a chevron argent three roses gules'. The crest on the helm supplied in the kit was a goat's head with long curving horns, so this would need to be remodelled. (A crest such as this would seem to be highly impractical in action, but there is some strong evidence to suggest that crests were worn on the battlefield - though how commonly is uncertain.) Sir Robert's type of body armour was known as 'a coat of plates' or sometimes 'a pair of plates'. The functional canvas garment that held the metal plates together would have been finished with a decorative covering of a richly coloured material such as velvet. The covering of Walter von Bopfingen's coat of plates is green, patterned with yellow crosses (see illustration). Evidence from England regarding the colour of these coverings comes from an inventory of the armour of the Earl of Hereford dated 1322: *'j peire des plates couvertes de vert velvet'* -

other armours are mentioned covered with *'drap d'or'* and *'rouge samyt'*.

I won't detail here how I assembled the castings of the figures, since I followed the procedures already described in Chapters 2 and 3, but will limit myself to the conversion and detailing work undertaken.

THE ARMING CAP & CREST

The arming cap in use at this time was probably a fairly simple affair, as the helm itself had an internal lining and a system of straps that supported it on the head. The helm did not rest directly on the shoulders, which allowed the head to move freely. It is often suggested that a bascinet and mail aventail was worn under the great helm, and there is evidence to support this. However, by the later 14th century the more elongated form of the bascinet makes this arrangement unlikely; so I think that by Knollys' time, if the helm was worn, it was directly over an arming cap. With a few contemporary references to hand that suggested the kind of headgear I was aiming to reconstruct, I began work on the castings. I cut away the decorated headband and all the detail above this, then drew the outline of an arming cap onto the head with the point of a scalpel. Then I used Milliput to build up the shape of the cap, and when it had cured I worked it into its final form with a knife and files.

I had in my scrap book a series of pictures of heraldic shields and crests from the famous *Armorial de Gelre* which was compiled in the latter part of the 14th century. There were several drawings of rams' heads in the armorial

and, most importantly, they were drawn in the style of the period. Rams seem to have been popular as crests all over Europe at this time, and many displayed a pair of 'wings' attached to the sides of the crest. The goat's head in the kit was a separate casting. I cut the long horns away and used Milliput to modify it to the appearance of a heraldic ram's head with suitable horns. This looked fine when in place on top of the helm. I decided that the helm itself, being held in the crook of the right arm, would be noticeably more effective if it were hollow.

HOLLOWING A HELMET

Not being in the habit of using power tools I had at first struggled to find enough uses for my recently purchased Expo Mini-Drill. However, hollowing out helms was one job that couldn't be done just as easily by hand; so the machine was connected up and I set about justifying its purchase. I started by drilling a short way into the bottom of the helm with a fine drill bit, then used increasingly larger bits until I could use a rough burr in the chuck and open out the hole. Progressing in this manner I removed the bulk of the metal. I intended to drill out the sights of the helm and the breathing holes, so the front of the helm needed to be carefully ground away inside to give an impression of thin metal; the back could be left relatively thick. I chucked a flat burr and achieved this result quite quickly. Then, putting aside the power drill, with a fine bit held in a pin chuck I drilled out the breathing holes and the sights by hand, which produced a remarkably realistic result.

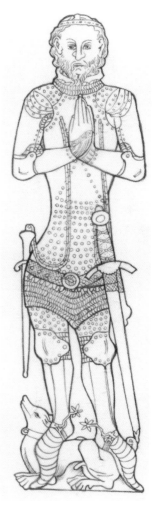

ABOVE Knollys' armour and weapons are based closely on contemporary evidence. One of the most remarkable sources is the brass of Ralph de Knevynton in the church at Aveley in Essex. Dated 1370, this depicts a fine 'coat of plates' with two chains hanging from the breastplate to secure the weapons. The armour bears a striking resemblance to that in the effigy of the German knight Walter von Bopfingen. (Author's drawing)

LEFT The effigy of Walter von Bopfingen, dating from 1359, survives in the church of St Blasius in Bopfingen, Baden-Wurtemberg. The colouring is probably a later restoration but may follow the original scheme. The four chains hanging from the breastplate were a German fashion, and have no parallel in English monumental art of the period. (Photo Hans Trauner)

ABOVE The base nears completion; an area of grass is taking shape on the right. I began by glueing down an area of grass mat; the edges were feathered into the surrounding groundwork, then the edge was covered with Milliput and textured with an old toothbrush. Finally a few random stones were added to break up the outline.

RIGHT The final mock-up stage; everything can be placed in position but can still be removed and taken to pieces for painting.

ABOVE Painting is underway in this view of the archer; you can see that the arrow crosses the bow just above the grip and at right angles to it. The top flight of the arrow is uppermost and the bowstring is taut.

THE GROUNDWORK

I wanted to model a 'busy' base displaying as much incidental detail as I could fit into the limited space without it seeming contrived. The base was a square of half-inch plywood which I thought was about the right size for the two figures to comfortably share. On this I built up the underlying relief structure with scraps of wood and card, then added the textured groundwork to this with Milliput. The two figures were then positioned by means of brass locating rods so that they could be removed when necessary as work progressed.

The two archers' stakes were positioned pointing outwards, then a broken sword, a dagger, a battered helm and a discarded gauntlet were bedded in place. The two shields and the banner were also positioned, but not fixed in place as they needed to be removed later for painting.

THE LONGBOWMAN

I didn't convert the longbowman in any way as he fitted my design as he was; but I did add a small bundle of arrows to his waist belt, and a leaden maul and billhook at his feet. The bundle of arrows was suggested by a Gerry Embleton drawing which caught my attention on a page illustrating medieval archery equipment. Modelling this detail would not only illustrate the way arrows were often carried, but would also create an effective diagonal accent to the pose of the figure.

I cast five white-metal arrows from one of the more useful moulds in the workshop,

LEFT AND BELOW LEFT Two views of the well-equipped mid-14th century bowman with all his archery gear. He wears a wicker and stiffened leather protective cap, and his green and white particoloured jacket identifies him as a Cheshire man. Over this he wears a sleeveless padded 'akheton' and an English livery jacket bearing the red cross of St George. He has a bag and water-gourd on his left hip, with an axe for close-quarter fighting; a purse, and a sheaf of arrows, hang at his right side (English archers did not wear quivers). The arrows may seem over-scale, but they aren't - the early 16th century arrows recovered from the *Mary Rose* confirm documentary evidence that the English war arrow was a heavy, massive missile.

trimmed the flights a little, and glued them together as closely as possible. Then I filled the gaps between the shafts with Milliput to make a solid structure, and made the bag into which the arrowheads fitted from the same material.

When assembling a figure with a longbow the difficulty is to align the bow, arrow and bowstring correctly so that the arrow passes over the handle of the bow at right angles, and the bowstring appears taught and in the correct plane in relation to the bow. When 'nocked' on the bowstring the arrow should have the top or vertical flight uppermost to ensure the smooth passage of the arrow over the bow. The top flight was sometimes marked or coloured differently to identify it. You can see how these arrangements should look in the accompanying photographs of the bowman under construction.

ABOVE The pewter banner with its Milliput fringe is displayed here on a page from my sketchbook. This contains some useful drawings which I use as a guide when painting heraldry. The lion rampant has been drawn on the yellow ground so that its extremities relate to the edges of the shield. This initial drawing should solve the crux of the problem; it remains only to refine the drawing now.

ABOVE The shield of William, Count of Namur lies damaged and discarded on the battlefield. I drilled two holes through the shield and glued arrows into these to suggest that this is the shield of a defeated foe.

ABOVE RIGHT Sir Robert Knollys' shield is propped against an archer's stake amidst the debris of battle. Drawing the correct geometrical shape of the tiny roses and getting the spacing right took several attempts.

THE SHIELDS & BANNER

The banner which I positioned behind Sir Robert Knollys is that of St George, which was carried in the field by all English armies at that time. The discarded shield on the ground behind him is that of William, Count of Namur; we know that this French nobleman fought at Crécy in 1346 and was still active in his king's service in the 1360s. The count's shield displays, on a gold or yellow field, a black lion rampant with a red crown and overall a red baton. This would be described in heraldic blason thus: 'Or, a lion rampant sable armed, langued and crowned sable, overall a baston gules'. The main thing to consider when painting a heraldic lion is that the beast must be drawn so that it relates to the shape of the shield. I first drew the position of the lion's body, legs and tail before I

RIGHT 'Sir Robert Knollys and an archer of his company, France 1369'.

LEFT The medieval knight in classic pose: Guillaume de Martel, Keeper of the Oriflamme, killed at the battle of Agincourt in 1415. This is a 54mm model by the Italian medievalist Mario Venturi. (Photo M. Venturi)

BELOW 'Scourge of the battlefield': 45 years after our Cheshire bowman followed Sir Robert Knollys across the Channel, an archer of a new generation stands at bay, ready to inflict the greatest defeat of all on the nobility of France at Agincourt. Adrian Bay's expressively posed longbowman - complete with lowered hose, which students of the campaign will understand - suggests the dramatic events about to unfold on that fateful autumn day in 1415. Adrian modelled the 80mm figure in Milliput and added cast weapons from the Border Miniatures range.

enlarged this into an outline of the lion. The drawing has to be right before you start to refine it into the finished state.

Robert Knollys' coat-of-arms, though it looks simple, was much more troublesome to paint - the three stylised roses had to be drawn the same size and in the right places on the white chevron, and it took several attempts to get it right. First I drew three 'boxes' on the chevron into which the roses or cinquefoils would fit. Once I had drawn these inside the boxes I painted the unwanted guidelines out, and was left with a drawing that only needed to be carefully filled in and have the leaves added.

You need a fine-pointed brush to draw with paint; my pricey Kolinsky 00 sable split as I was drawing the lion, and though it would have been perfect for parallel lines and double-tailed lions, I had to tame it with the scissors. This luckily produced a fine lining brush with which to add the darker detail inside the outline of the roses.

The banner of St George was made from sheet pewter which was glued round a 1/16in brass rod and topped with a white-metal finial. The banner was then edged with Milliput which was textured with a knife blade to produce the tassels and fringes. I didn't make any folds in the banner, as they seem to have been stiffened, but I could have done so at this stage before the putty hardened completely.

HERALDRY IN MEDIEVAL ENGLAND

ABOVE 'Ermine, two bars gemel gules': Walter Huntercome's shield is taken from the Lord Marshall's Roll of about 1310. There are a variety of ways of representing the ermine tails but in this case the medieval artist has drawn them in a particularly lively manner.

Heraldry served to identify an armoured knight on the battlefield, and in medieval times it was a very simple and direct artform. This section is not a heraldry lesson, but rather a short working introduction for the guidance of modellers which might spark an interest in the subject. It is really only necessary for modelmakers to know a few basic heraldic terms, but it is essential to have good reference material. Luckily there is nowadays an increasing amount of published material available to enable modellers to research an appropriate coats-of-arms and to avoid the use of 'bogus and imaginary heraldry'. No good bookshelf should be without a heraldry title, but general works often contain little of immediate practical use to modellers. However, among the titles listed in the Bibliography readers will find several which catalogue the knights who fought in particular battles and describe their coats-of-arms.

The forerunners of medieval heraldic charges can be glimpsed briefly in the 11th century Bayeaux Tapestry where some of the contingents present in Duke William's army are identified by the devices on their flags, though the various shield designs depicted are not true heraldry. It was not until the end of the following century that a recognisable and hereditary system evolved by which individuals could be identified. In England a coat-of-arms was the preserve of an individual person, and though the basic design might identify a particular family the 'undifferenced' arms were only carried by the head of the family. For instance, the blue lion rampant of the Percy Earls of Northumberland was unique to the earl himself; his sons and other members of the family had to add a 'difference' to the arms - as illustrated by 'Hotspur' on the opposite page.

In England heraldry was the exclusive prerogative of the nobility, knighthood and landed gentry, over which a College of Heralds evolved to regulate affairs. Regulation was obviusly necessary if the arms were to serve efficiently as identification. In the 14th century the art of heraldry was in its purest form; the uncluttered coats-of-arms served simply and directly to identify the fighting men. Towards the end of the medieval period coats-of-arms became increasingly complicated, for instance by the 'quarterings' reflecting intermarriage between armigerous families; and as the confusion increased so the art of heraldry declined.

I have tried to illustrate most of the terms mentioned in this section, but heraldry abounds in terminology, and to make matters worse the 'naming of parts' is in old French. I have indicated where examples are shown pictorially in other parts of the book, but you may have to look some terms up yourself. I have not enlarged upon obvious terms such as 'roundel' or 'cross'.

THE HERALDIC SHIELD

The shield is always described from the point of view of the bearer so that the right or dexter side of the shield coincides with the bearer's right hand - i.e. the opposite way round from the observer's view. In the arms of Richard Pembridge (see illustration on page 64, item v), 'Barry of six or and azure, a bend gules', the bend goes from the bearer's top right of the shield to bottom left. In heraldic terms left is sinister, so a 'bend sinister' would go from the bearer's top left to bottom right.

Barry is one of the simple ways of dividing the shield, and is the term used to describe horizontal bars or stripes. If these stripes were vertical then the pattern would be termed *paly*. Other simple divisions are *checky* (see the arms of Robert Clifford in Chapter 3), and *quarterly*, i.e. divided into quarters.

HERALDIC COLOURS

Colours in heraldry are divided into the 'metals' - gold and silver, and the 'tinctures' - red, blue and black. Purple and green were little used until the later 15th century.

The essential rule of heraldry is that a colour is never placed on a colour, always on a metal; and conversely a metal is never placed on a metal, always on a colour.

In addition to the above there are two 'furs'- ermine and vair. Ermine was the stoat's white winter coat with the black tail tips sewn on. Vair, from the Latin *varus*, varied,

LEFT Fiery-tempered Henry Percy, known as 'Hotspur', differenced his arms from those of his father the Earl of Northumberland with a 'label of three points gules'. He was defeated and captured by the Scots at Otterburn in 1388. In 1402, in a reversal of fortune, he and his father inflicted a crushing defeat on the Scots at Homildon Hill in Northumberland. In the following year he was killed at the battle of Shrewsbury while in revolt against Henry IV. The Armorial de Gelre contains a drawing of the arms and crest of the Percys, and it was from this source that I sculpted the 'cap of maintenance' and the lion crest. The lion on the front of Hotspur's heraldic jupon faces towards our left, so the lion on the rear would too.

Some knights who fought at the battle of Crécy in 1346. These coats-of-arms display the simple heraldry in use in the middle of the 14th century.

(i) Sir James Audley - 'Gules fretty or, a label azure'.

(ii) Sir Guy Bryan - 'Or, three piles conjoined in point azure'.

(iii) Sir John Paveley - 'Azure, a cross patonce or, in the first quarter a martlet argent'.

(iv) Sir Thomas Wingfield - 'Argent, on a bend gules cottised sable three pairs of wings argent'.

(v) Sir Richard Pembridge - 'Barry of six or and azure, a bend gules'.

(vi) Sir Reginald Cobham - 'Gules, on a chevron or three estoiles sable'.

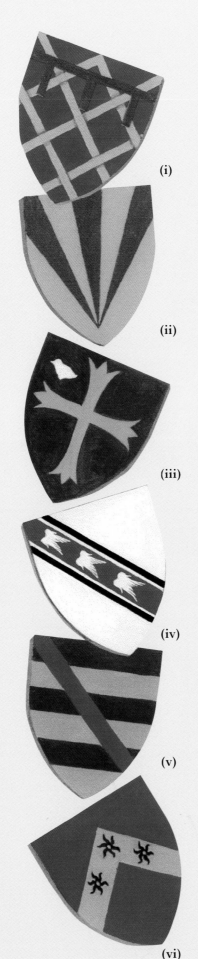

(i)

(ii)

(iii)

(iv)

(v)

(vi)

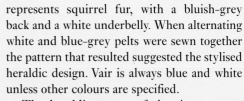

represents squirrel fur, with a bluish-grey back and a white underbelly. When alternating white and blue-grey pelts were sewn together the pattern that resulted suggested the stylised heraldic design. Vair is always blue and white unless other colours are specified.

The heraldic names of the tinctures are summarised thus:

Gold or yellow	*or*
Silver or white	*argent*
Blue	*azure*
Red	*gules*
Black	*sable*
Green	*vert*
Purple	*perpure*

There are no rules to determine which pigment should be used to represent these tinctures, but some guidance can be given. It would not be wrong to use metallic gold and silver paint for *or* and *argent*, but I think it is best to use yellow and white paint to represent the metals when painting coats of arms in miniature. A good heraldic yellow should avoid any hint of lemon and tend more towards the orange end of the spectrum; Naples Yellow or Cadmium Yellow work well. *Argent* can be painted a little off-white to allow it to tone in with the rest of the model. *Gules* should be Scarlet or Vermilion; and *sable* is simply black. *Azure* can be painted Ultramarine or Cerulean Blue, but these should not be used straight from the tube; they need to be lightened with a little white. *Vert* should be Emerald Green. The less common *perpure* should tend neither towards blue nor red, and again needs to be lightened.

DEVICES & CHARGES

The devices that are painted on shields are called charges, and it helps to know the terms used for some of the common ones. Those most often encountered are the simple geometric shapes known as 'ordinaries'. Among these are the *chief* (Chapter 2, Menzies); *fess* (Chapter 3, Clifford); *chevron* (Crécy shields herewith, item vi, Cobham); *bend* (item iv, Wingfield); *saltire* (Chapter 6, Neville); *cross*; *pile* (item ii, Bryan); and *canton* (page 68, Lancaster).

These can also be drawn with an ornamental edge; thus they are often *embattled* like battlements, *wavy*, *dancetty* (herewith, item viii, Deincourt) or *engrailed* with a scalloped edge (herewith, item ix, Loring, with a 'bend engrailed sable').

Another group of common charges are the 'subordinaries', though I am not sure that the term was current in medieval times. These are

| (vii) | (viii) | (ix) |

really just more simple geometric shapes. They include the *bordure* or border; *tressure, lozenge, fret, billet, annulet* or ring, *roundel, orle* and *inescutcheon*. The arms of Thomas Erpingham (item vii above) illustrate the last two charges.

HERALDIC ANIMALS & EVERYDAY OBJECTS

The lion, being the king of beasts and symbolising strength and nobility, is by far the most popular of animate charges. It appears on shields in a variety of postures, but the lion rampant is most often portrayed. The lion is also commonly depicted as passant, crowned, or double-tailed; and is confusingly termed a leopard if portrayed passant guardant as in the arms of England. An instance of the popularity of the lion as a knightly charge can be discovered in the *Rime of Caerlaverock*, which describes the arms of 105 knights who accompanied Edward I on his Scottish expedition of 1300; fully a quarter feature a lion in one form or other.

Birds, such as the imperious eagle or the raven (corbie) and parrot (popinjay) are used less often. The curious martlet, which is usually drawn without legs, is probably the most common of all birdlike charges. Fish and sea-shells occasionally appear as charges, as do objects taken from everyday life: crescents and stars, spurs, various flowers, buckets, fetter-locks and hunting horns are all to be seen.

HERALDIC STYLE

The style in which charges were drawn on shields in medieval times should be considered carefully, and this is an area where some

original research could be undertaken. Medieval 'rolls of arms' are often 'blasoned' or in the form of written documents, but some are illustrated with painted heraldic shields and these are worth some detailed examination.

Rolls such as the mid-13th century 'Matthew Paris Shields' or the later 'Lord Marshall's Roll' of about 1310 illustrate, in the style of the day, the arms of many prominent personalities. The charges are drawn in a simple, sometimes quirky yet always lively style, which could be profitably employed by modellers to convey a feel of the right century

ABOVE Arms of three other famous English knights.
(vii) Sir Thomas Erpingham, who commanded the archers at Agincourt - 'Vert, an inescutcheon within an orle of martlets argent'.
(viii) Sir William Deincourt, who was killed at Bannockburn - 'Azure billetty and a fess dancetty or'.
(ix) Sir Nigel Loring - 'Quarterley argent and gules a bend engrailed sable'. This is the historical knight whom Arthur Conan Doyle took as his inspiration for his two amusing novels of medieval adventure, *Sir Nigel* and *The White Company*.

LEFT I photographed this shield with a fine lion rampant carved in relief in a church in North Yorkshire. The knight holding the shield was in an awkward, dark recess and was rather plain, but seemed by the style of his armour to date from about 1400.

Le Counte de Arundell

in their own painted heraldry. The lions rampant of the latter roll are nearer to a Jack Russell than they are to the King of Beasts, and demonstrate that no knowledge of leonine anatomy is necessary to draw the heraldic lion.

ROYAL HERALDRY

About 1195 Richard I of England had a new Great Seal cut which shows him mounted and displaying three lions passant guardant on his shield. This is the first appearance of the Royal Arms of England, and they remain the same to this day. In medieval times a lion passant guardant was often termed a leopard; so in 1340, when Edward III claimed the French throne, we hear that he quartered the 'leopards' of England with the 'lilies' of France. Originally the lilies or *fleurs de lys* covered the whole surface of the French Royal Banner in an all-over pattern, but Charles V reduced their number to three. The original pattern of lilies is known as 'France Ancient'; the later design with just three lilies is called 'France Modern'. King Henry IV of England followed suit in 1405, and changed his banner accordingly.

THE ORIGINS OF COATS-OF-ARMS

It is rarely clear how knights chose the design of their arms; however, in the case of 'canting' or punning arms the origins of some devices can be seen. Some of these are simple and obvious, such as the well-known calves of

Hugh Calveley; similarly the wings displayed on the arms of Sir John Wingfield, and the trumpets on the arms of Roger de Trumpington 'cant' on the names of the bearers. There are many of these plays on words so typical of the medieval mind; Corbet bears ravens; Fauconer, falcons; and Swinburne, boars' heads.

Many coats-of-arms must have originated by chance or caprice, the bends, chequers and bars forming simple distinctive patterns which made for easy recognition of men armed for battle. Some knights took as their arms devices similar to their overlord. In Cheshire, for instance, the Earls of Chester bore garbs or wheatsheaves; so in response many of the knights of the locality took the wheatsheaves as their own, simply differencing their arms with different colours and arrangements of the charges. In Westmorland the de Lancaster barons of Kendal bore the arms 'Argent, two barres gules and a lion passant or in a canton gules'. Their feudal neighbours took the same basic arms but adopted a different charge from the lion in the canton; thus the Derwentwaters took a rose, the Preston family a cinquefoil and the Kirkbys a mullet or star.

BLASON & TRICK

'Blasoning' is the way a herald would describe a coat-of-arms in terminology that was understood throughout Western Europe. To read or translate a blason we need to know how the description works and in which order it is set out. The field or background colour is described first. If the field is divided vertically (per-pale) or quartered (quarterly), or if the field is sprinkled with small charges (semé), then this must be stated. The charges are then described in a logical sequence in much the same order as a painter would paint the devices onto the field. Similarly if the charges were being appliquéd to a banner or surcoat they would be sewn down in much the same sequence as they were blasoned.

When the coat-of-arms is illustrated by means of an annotated diagram then this is known as a 'trick of arms' or 'tricking'.

CRESTS

Various crests were in use as early as the 12th century, but the true three-dimensional crest did not appear until the beginning of the 14th century. These true heraldic crests were often fantastic pieces of sculpture, designed not for

LEFT King Henry V and his standard bearer Sir John Codrington under the Royal Banner at the battle of Agincourt, 1415. The Royal Arms of England are quartered with France Modern. The figures are from Marco Lucchetti's Soldiers range and were sculpted and painted by Mario Venturi.

RIGHT The arms of de Lancaster: 'Argent, two barres gules and a lion passant or in a canton gules'.

use on the battlefield but for display in tournaments and pageants. They were lightweight constructions made of such materials as moulded leather *(cuir-bouilli)*, papier maché or thin wood. Sometimes a wicker framework was employed, and feathers were often used with these frameworks to create splendid plumed *panaches*. Though some crests are directly related to charges appearing on the knights' shield - e.g. the calf's head crest of Hugh Calveley - there are many that are quite unconnected; that of Robert Knollys is an example. Helmets often had a decorative cloth mantling; these were generally in the main colour of the knight's arms with the lining being the colour of the main metal or fur.

RIGHT The stylised calves of Calveley are carved in relief on Sir Hugh's heraldic jupon; the bovine charges and the calf's head crest, on which Sir Hugh's head rests, are a 'cant' or pun on his name.

CHAPTER 5

THE CASTLE

THE PROJECT

The sporadic outbursts of fighting in late 15th century England between the Royal Houses of Lancaster and York became known as the Wars of the Roses. These uncertain times of conflict provide the setting for the modelling project described in this chapter and the next. The model featured in various stages of construction has as its centrepiece the famous Earl of Warwick, Richard Neville, known to history as 'The Kingmaker'. He is mounted on a caparisoned horse and is clad in a complete harness of plate armour. With his heraldic standard aloft he is emerging from a castle gateway accompanied by armed retainers.

This chapter will concentrate on the construction of the castle; Chapter 6 will describe the figure modelling involved.

RESEARCH & BACKGROUND

I came upon the imposing castle of Caher in County Tipperary quite by chance while meandering across the south of Ireland on a hill-walking holiday a few summers ago. Its discovery set my imagination afire and was the starting point for this model. The largely 15th century fortification was built by the Butlers, Earls of Ormonde, engulfing the earlier 13th century O'Brien stronghold. Caher is the largest 15th century castle in Ireland, and has been restored sensitively by the Irish authorities (for which I was grateful, as it saved me the job when I came to build it in model form).

Surprisingly, the castle does not display any particularly Irish architectural features; the characteristic battlements of Irish fortified buildings are absent, and there is little to distinguish Caher from an English stronghold. The Irish countryside is liberally dotted with a surprising wealth of well-preserved but little-known castles and fortified tower houses just waiting to be discovered by the enthusiast of the unusual.

My aim was to model the gateway at Caher Castle through which a mounted knight had issued with supporting foot soldiers, so I needed to incorporate a section of wall on both sides of the gate to provide an ample setting for the figures. I decided that discipline was needed, however, and that I should limit myself to undertaking what was possible within the time I could reasonably spare. The temptation to keep adding a bit more wall here and the odd incident and detail there was hard to resist. It began to grow quite out of control in an almost organic manner, and was soon twice the size of the model that I had planned. Similar building and detailing methods to those used in Chapter 2 are employed in this project, so only the new techniques employed will be described in any detail.

As I am using 80mm figures the scale expressed as a ratio is 1:23, or as a linear scale 13mm = 1 foot. I calculated that this meant that the flanking tower would be about 18ins high. I started work on a 14in square base made of three-quarter-inch blockboard, which seemed a generous enough stage for the scene I had in mind. Ultimately, although the model only gained a couple of inches in width, the introduction of additional structures extended the overall length to over 2 feet 6 inches.

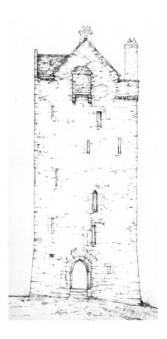

ABOVE Drawing from my sketchbook of Drumharsna Castle in County Galway - one of the many fascinating fortified buildings awaiting discovery in the Irish countryside.

LEFT The fortified gateway leading into the inner ward at Castle Caher, Co. Tipperary, was a 15th century architectural gem; it stirred my imagination, and I knew immediately that it would make a perfect setting for a group of medieval figures. I took a series of photos of the gate from every angle possible, and made a few measurements to help establish other heights and widths later.

RIGHT On the left of this rear view of the group of buildings centring on the gateway is the battlemented flanking tower. The stair tower has a long arrow-slit which threatens the wall walk from which the photo was taken. Between the stair tower and the tall keep on the right can be seen the gatehouse - with three ascending arrow-slits - which houses the portcullis mechanism.

RIGHT The extent of the section of model castle as originally envisaged. Plywood and blockboard sheet, softwood sections and card were used to establish a strong underlying basic structure. The walls have been textured in a similar manner to that described in Chapter 2. From this nucleus the model expanded in all directions as new ideas occurred to me.

FAR RIGHT A rear view of the structure showing the haphazard yet solid method of construction, and the variety of wooden sections and thick card used.

WINDOWS & GLAZING

A leaded window in the flanking tower overlooks the courtyard, its square head and label moulding identifying it as a later insertion which could not be earlier than the late 15th century. I thought the style might have been a bit late to include, but I decided to chance it and model the window and its glazing as it exists.

I cut the shape of the window opening in the tower and edged the inside with strip wood to give it depth. The label moulding above was cut from card and glued onto the lintel; then this and the surrounding stonework were chamfered with a scalpel. I decided to hinge the glazed part of the window, even if this feature was a little ahead of its time, to provide the opportunity to create incident in the window opening.

A section of 5mm square etched brass fret formed the basis of the leaded window. I tinned this on both sides with a high tin content solder; then fused horizontal brass strengthening rods on to the back, and a

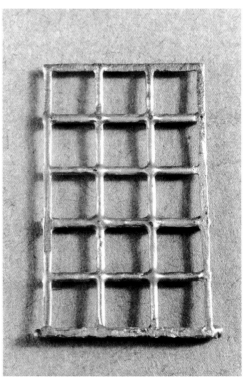

FAR LEFT A close-up view of the overhanging structure which defends the gateway. The triangular supports were carved from strip wood, then the arched facade was added from thin ply of the correct scale thickness. The arrow-slit was not pierced through the wall as I intended to paint it in realistically later.

LEFT The window in the flanking tower under construction. The lateral strengthening rods have been soldered to the back of the brass fret, and a strip of clear acetate lies in place.

FAR LEFT The front of the brass fret was tinned with solder; then relief was built up in very low-melt solder to suggest the shape of the lead glazing bars.

LEFT The finished section of leaded glazing is set in a wooden frame, which may have been removed from the opening and replaced with a shutter at night.

slightly over-length vertical rod on the edge to act as a hinge. The front of this assembly was then coated with low-melt solder to give an impression of the profile of the leaded window bars. Thin acetate sheet was glued in place behind the fret - with an accidental flood of super-glue, which completely covered both the acetate and the glazing bars. The accident proved fortuitous, as I discovered that when this dried out the acetate resembled the small panes of uneven, rather opaque glass used in the 15th century.

A SERIES OF COURTYARDS

It was at this stage that I realised I would have to address the problem of the space behind the gateway, since this was not only visible but was a focal point of the model. I could have resorted to the use of a painted backdrop behind the gate, but I decided that an enclosed courtyard similar to the one on my plan of Caher would present interesting possibilities. This first enclosed yard had an arched gateway in the rear wall, which again presented me with a similar dilemma. The second gateway led in

turn into a further courtyard area bounded by buildings. I decided to model this area too, as these spaces would provide both a stage for incidental detail and a context for the weapons and equipment which I planned to model.

THE FIRST COURTYARD

This area was entered at Caher Castle through the fortified gateway, and was bounded by the high wall of the keep on one side and by the outer perimeter wall on the other. The gateway from this courtyard led into the inner ward, but I had no photographs of the gate nor of the open space beyond it. I needed an enclosed rather than an open area, so I decided to improvise this section of the model by introducing part of a building from elsewhere to serve as a finite boundary. My photos of Aydon Castle in Northumberland provided me with an example of a small gateway of the right period to work from (see Research & Fieldwork section, page 18).

THE SECOND COURTYARD & THE YETT

The basic structure of this area of the model was simply two pieces of thick card glued at right angles to each other and supported by strip wood. The reference I used for this area was a photograph of an inner wall at Aydon Castle, which I scanned into the computer and sized so that the print-out could be glued in place to form the end wall. The result of the experiment, especially when the door and

ABOVE An unsuspecting kitchen cat strolls home across the yard, unaware of approaching nemesis as an anonymous hand empties the 'night soil' from the window high above.

RIGHT This photo taken at Castle Caher provided useful information when I added the battlements to the flanking tower. The series of rectangular holes level with the wallhead may be 'put-log holes' which were used in the erection of a wooden hoarding or 'warhead', projecting outward from the wall to serve as a fighting platform.

window openings were cut out, was surprisingly acceptable, and as the print was on ordinary paper it was quite easy to work on it with acrylic paints. I thought that this was a technique probably best restricted to a small area, however, as too much printed stonework could lead to a dolls' house appearance.

I deepened the door and window openings with card surrounds, then glazed the window in a similar manner to that in the tower described above. The head of the doorway at Aydon was identical to the one that I had found so striking at Naworth Castle, though the latter doorway still retained an ageing yet purposeful iron 'yett'. I thought that the inclusion of this feature would give the doorway a strong presence and add an air of brooding menace to the model (see Research & Fieldwork section, page 18). The construction of the yett is detailed in the captions to the accompanying photographs.

THE FLANKING TOWER

I next turned my attention to the curved section of tower that flanked the main gateway. I had originally planned this to be merely a facade, but I decided to extend the height to the battlements; then I noticed a cardboard tube in my box room that was about the right diameter to use as a stair tower, so I added this to the composition too. This meant that I now had the basic structure of half of the cylindrical tower in place. I had intended to leave it at that, but every time I looked at the tower it demanded to be completed in its

entirety - so I built the rest of it... .

The card skin of the tower was supported inside by a series of disks of thin plywood, which were in turn held in place by strip wood. I used quite thin card, which bent easily, for the outer skin, preferring to use two thin layers if necessary rather than thicker material which might crack or become angular on bending.

The curved battlements were crenellated and pierced with shot-holes, so they needed to appear three-dimensional throughout

(Continued on page 76)

LEFT The flanking tower is growing upwards as the battlements are added to the wallhead and the stair tower's conical roof takes shape. The groundwork is also advancing, as I try to add interest and variety to the expanse of open space in the foreground.

FAR LEFT The tall curved battlements had to appear three-dimensional, so they were made with an outer and an inner skin. The capstones were cut into sections as they had to curve to follow the shape of the battlements. The card tube which forms the stair tower can be seen with the supporting structure for its conical roof in place.

LEFT In this rear view you can see in place the wooden strips on to which the inner skin of the battlements will be glued. The roof is in place on the stair tower, and adjoining this layers of thin card curve round to form the base of the flanking tower.

RIGHT Red lentils vary in size and shape, so they have a look of the real thing when used to represent a cobbled surface. The lentils are first glued in place in a random manner as seen in this view. Ready-mixed household filler is then spread over them, and as it dries the excess is brushed off to leave the lentils looking like cobbles set in earth.

FAR RIGHT The layout of the series of courtyards is explained by this view through the fortified gateway. The two inner yards are still at an early stage of construction, but already the viewer's interest is drawn inwards to the far doorway.

RIGHT The portcullis (French, *porte*, a door, and *coulisse*, a groove). Lengths of square section softwood strip were made into a grid by means of cross-halving joints. The bottoms of the vertical members were carefully pointed; then the assembly was cut to shape to fit into the groove in the pointed archway. The portcullis slid vertically in this groove and is modelled in the raised position, when most of it was inside the gatehouse above. You can see the lines that mark the position of a series of slots on the left of the wooden model; on the right the slots have been sawn and pointed brass rods have been glued into them.

FAR LEFT The underlying plywood structure of the first courtyard can be seen in this view of the early stages of construction. The texture of the stonework is being built up using the methods described in Chapter 2.

LEFT A view through the second gateway to show the building in the third courtyard at an early stage of construction. I sloped the groundwork upwards so that I could raise the doorway to the height at which it worked best when viewed through the two gateways.

FAR LEFT The real doorway at Aydon Castle. The photograph was scanned on my computer and printed to scale to see if this way of achieving instant masonry was effective. The irregular cobbles and uneven surface of the yard seen here provided a useful reference.

LEFT The limited extent of the modelled third courtyard can be seen here. The printed stonework has been glued on to modelling card, and the openings for the door and window have been cut out. A brass fret has been cut to size to represent the leaded window, and work is underway to deepen the doorway.

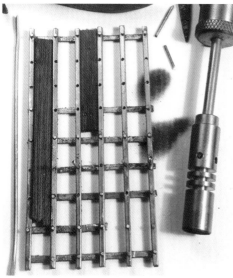

their circuit. I made these in the manner of a modern interior partition wall, with an inner structure of square section strip wood and a thin outer skin of card. First I glued the outer face of the battlements in place on to the roof level of the tower; then I drew the shape of the crenellations and shot-holes onto this. Upright strip wood spacers were glued behind this facing, some being placed so that they would edge the openings, which I cut out when the liberally applied glue had dried. I finished off the structure with a curved card parapet with triangular capstones which topped the battlements. Finally I filled any unwanted gaps with card scraps; and textured the structure to represent stonework, in the usual way.

LEFT The horizontals are all soldered in place. The wooden boards are being used as temporary spacers to position the uprights while holes are drilled to take short lengths of brass rod which will hold the structure together. Some of these rods can be seen in place, and others have already been soldered in and filed down to represent the uneven rivets of the original.

THE STAIR TOWER ROOF

My photos of Caher suggested that the stair tower, which was built on to the flanking tower and housed the spiral stair giving access to its floors, was capped by a conical slated roof. In order to model this feature a series of triangular shapes was glued on top of the tube that formed the stair tower, to support a stiff paper cone that would carry the slates. Conical roof slates are small and tapered to allow them to lie around the shape of the roof, and towards the apex they are very small indeed. I made the lower courses of slates by cutting tiny shapes from cartridge

LEFT The construction of the yett is complete, and only a few areas of exposed brass still need to be painted. On the right of the door can be seen a simple crossbow, made by Keith Durham from Milliput and twisted wire. The real bow was spanned by placing one foot in the stirrup and pulling back the bowstring either by hand or with the aid of a belt-hook til it engaged with a rotating ivory nut.

Dry-brushing the rough texture of the groundwork and large areas of masonry wore down my brushes alarmingly. After demolishing an expensive hog-bristle Windsor & Newton in no time at all, I bought half a dozen of the cheapest bristle brushes I could find. These proved quite adequate for this rough work, and though the dry-brushing reduced them to a sorry state they still had some life left as glue brushes. Brushes in this state were useful to apply the copious quantities of glue and interior quality masonry paint that were used to texture the model (and some of them were eventually transformed into tufts of 'long grass').

The groundwork, castle walls and slate roofs, everything in fact, were painted with matt enamel colours. I employed a restrained palette and a dry-brushing technique, similar to that described in Chapter 2. I took a section of the building at a time and worked each to a finish, though care had to be taken to mask off completed areas when working on an adjacent section. I painted the masonry of the castle a reddish sandstone colour to contrast with the brown earthy hues of the groundwork and the grey of the slate roofs.

THE WEATHER VANE

It is likely that 'vane' is corrupted from the French word *fane* and that this derives from *fanion*, a flag. Vanes have been a traditional means of displaying armorial devices since the 13th century, and the conical roof of the stair tower demanded one to top it off. I had a picture of a splendid heraldic vane in a general book on heraldry (which was almost worth the price for that page alone – see under Stephen Friar in Bibliography) and I used this as the basis for my model.

The first and most crucial stage in making the vane was to draw the shape onto a thin sheet of brass using a knife blade against a steel rule. I cut this shape out with a piercing saw, then filed the edges down to the marked lines. A brass rod was tapered by using the Mini-Drill (see Chapter 1) to form the pole on which the vane turned. A thinner rod was cut to fit the slot in the top of the vane; then the assembly was soldered together. The hinges on which the vane turned and the rivets were added from modelling putty to complete the model.

ABOVE **An atmospheric view of the yett seen through the arch of the inner courtyard. Although there are no figures in view the prowling castle cat and an upturned bucket provide an immediate 'visual story'.**

paper and gluing them side by side, then overlapping them with the course above.

Towards the top the slates in the final courses proved too minute for this treatment and the roof threatened to get out of control. I reverted to using Milliput, and finished the final section of roof to the apex by impressing a suggestion of courses of tiny slates into a thin skin of the soft modelling putty. The final tiny courses were not modelled in relief as I thought these could probably be painted in successfully at a later stage. A final unifying texture was given to the roof with two liberal coats of interior quality textured paint. I used a mixture of black, yellow and white to make the grey of the roof tiles - a straight black and white mix can result in a dull and lifeless colour.

LEFT The arms of the Butler Earls of Ormonde decorate the vane now proudly topping the stair tower roof. A lone armoured sentinel watches over the castle approaches from the wallhead.

LEFT The brass weather vane is seen here cleaned up and ready to paint. The materials from which it is made are clearly distinguishable.

DRESSING THE SET: SOME MEDIEVAL WEAPONS

RIGHT A crossbow with cranequin, sallet and quiver were assembled and soldered together to form an attractive group of related objects. This 'still life with crossbow' was glued to a base, then modelled into the groundwork with Milliput. Note the characteristic shape of the fur-covered quiver in which the wooden-fletched crossbow bolts were carried heads upmost; and the thick composite bowstring, whipped with twine at the centre and ends. Crossbows were quite often carried by horsemen. There was no recoil, and it was possible to reload in the saddle; even so, bowmen nearly always dismounted to fight.

Medieval sources show a wondrous variety of shapes and sizes of weaponry, and those displayed around the castle courtyards in our model are only a small sample of the many possibilities. They are all made or derived from my own range of white metal oddments and accessories. Eduard Wagner illustrated a useful book in the 1950s (see Bibliography) which contains page after page of weapons and other fascinating and curious artefacts derived from medieval sources to tempt the creative modeller.

There were several varieties of medieval crossbow which differed mainly in the power of the bow and the way in which the string was drawn back. The simplest type, which was spanned by hand or with a belt-hook, can be seen on page 77 leaning against the wall by the iron yett. Powerful steel bows first appeared in about 1370 and increasingly replaced the earlier composite bows. These needed a mechanical device to bend the bow: either a 'goat's foot' lever, a hand-cranked cranequin ratchet bar, or a windlass with a set of pulleys and cords. As advances in technology added to the power of the crossbow it became increasingly complicated and slow to reload. However, a crossbow could be shot effectively without the physical strength and years of constant practice demanded by the longbow. In fact, because of the ease with which it handled and the lack of recoil it was a favourite with the ladies, who preferred it for the hunt.

Crude 'hand cannons' mounted on poles were in use during the 14th century, and handguns with an attached 'serpentine' lever combining a match-holder and a simple trigger appeared from early in the 1400s. By the 1460s quite large numbers of hand-gunners were commonplace in European armies and city militias; the army of the Dukes of Burgundy, one of the most professional in Europe, had equal numbers of hand-gunners, crossbowmen and pikemen by 1473.

LEFT All the gear you need to shoot a crossbow - here, the most powerful type of 15th century sprung steel bow. The pavise displays the livery colours and ragged staff badge of the Earl of Warwick; loading the crossbow took some time, and it was a good idea to do this in safety behind the propped pavise. The windlass, which hangs by its cords over the pavisse, was fitted onto the butt of the crossbow stock; then two hooks on the other end of the extended cords - here out of sight behind the pavise - were engaged with the bowstring, which was drawn back to engage the locking nut by winding the windlass handles. When modelling this group I soldered the windlass to the pavise, then passed waxed threads through holes drilled either side of the pulley wheels and carried them over the top of the pavise. Also note here the aiming device on the butt of the bowstock; the thumb of the right hand was placed in one of the diagonal grooves so that the top of the knuckle served as a backsight.

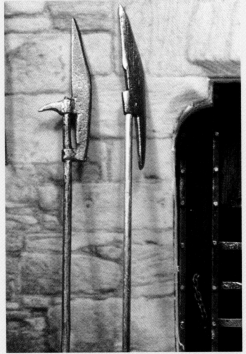

LEFT Two types of 'Jedart axe', a polearm much favoured on the Border and in Scotland; that on the right has been left unfinished to show the assembly stage. The axe-head was carved from a pewter blank, then a socket was drilled in this to take a spigot on the brass shaft. The base of the blade was then fastened to the shaft with a metal reinforcement to stabilise the structure. The finished poleaxe can be seen in photographs in the next chapter.

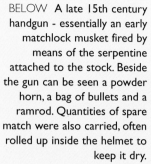

BELOW A late 15th century handgun - essentially an early matchlock musket fired by means of the serpentine attached to the stock. Beside the gun can be seen a powder horn, a bag of bullets and a ramrod. Quantities of spare match were also carried, often rolled up inside the helmet to keep it dry.

ABOVE A detail of one of my paintings from which the 'still-life' group developed. You can see a model of this little terrier included elsewhere, too.

CHAPTER 6
'THE KINGMAKER' – RICHARD NEVILLE, EARL OF WARWICK

THE PROJECT

The conversion work undertaken in this chapter, though more advanced than that described previously, should be within the capabilities of the average modeller if the simple methods described here are used. The mounted knight provides a fine opportunity for a display of late 15th century heraldry, and this subject will be considered in relation to shields, standards, banners, surcoats and caparisons.

THE CAPARISONED HORSE

A little research turned up a good many illustrations of caparisoned horses in medieval painting and sculpture as well as those on heraldic seals. This was an essential first stage before the modelling work even began and though no single image could provide all the information I needed, I kept them to hand throughout the modelling work as they provided a stimulation rather than a model to copy directly. I needed the folds of the covering to fall in such a way as to be in harmony with the movement of the horse; and I wanted to retain the feel of the dynamism of the animal underneath the drapery. I had some photos of Pilkington Jackson's fine statue of Robert the Bruce at Bannockburn; these demonstrated how even in a static pose a caparisoned horse could retain movement and vitality

The horse from the mounted kit I used was posed in a manner best suited for me to achieve these aims, and the vital movement of the animal helped to suggest the manner in which the folds in the drapery would fall. It seems unlikely that the caparison had any value as a defence against weapons in itself, and though it may be that some form of soft padded armour or even mail was sometimes present underneath I decided that, as I had no real evidence, I would not attempt to suggest this.

So much for what had to be done; now, how to do it? Milliput is the best and quickest medium for conveying the movement of drapery, but it needs some sort of support while it hardens. I cleaned up the castings of the horse halves first, scraping off the very fine mould lines with a scalpel (even horse halves,

which can be a problem for manufacturers to cast, should have no more than a vestigial mould mark). Next I soldered the armoured head and neck to the right hand horse half from the inside. Soldering horses together is a straightforward business, as they are composed of large, chunky castings.

(Continued on page 86)

ABOVE 'The Kingmaker'. In 1471 Warwick's shifting allegiance found him on the wrong side at the battle of Barnet, where in the confusion of the Lancastrian defeat the earl was killed before he could get to his horse.

RIGHT The right hand horse assembly is half embedded in Plastilene (not Plasticene) in this view. The shape of the inside of the caparison has been built up and marked out by scribing the Plastilene.

RIGHT The front of the caparison has been modelled in Milliput over the Plastilene support. Note the turned-back front corner, to give an impression of lightness and movement.

RIGHT The basic shape of the caparison is complete. When this assembly has hardened it can be removed from the Plastilene support and worked to its finished form.

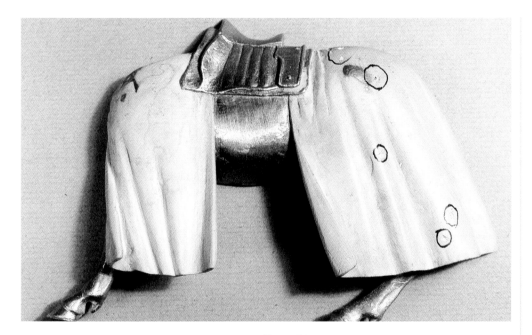

LEFT The work of refining the caparison is at an advanced stage; the black circles identify blemishes that need to be filled.

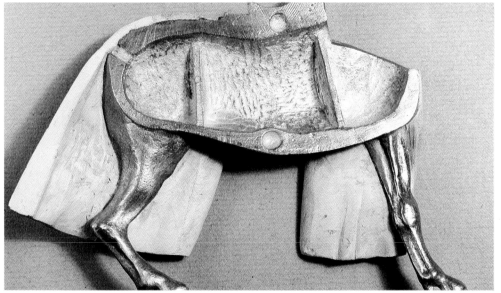

LEFT The left hand horse half showing the detail on the inside.

LEFT The finished caparison, saddlery and reins in place; the final loop of the reins will be added to the top of the rider's right hand at a late stage.

The caparison now comprised four quarters, and though I was fairly sure at this stage where the folds in the drapery were going, I didn't know how long it would take to complete each section. I initially mixed just enough Milliput for one of the front sections, and thumbed it firmly into place over both the casting and the Plastilene former (which proved resistant to this pressure, and retained its shape). The main folds were pressed into the soft modelling putty using the round, tapering shape of a paintbrush handle. These were generous folds, which would enable the heraldry to be drawn on later without too many problems. A few smaller creases were modelled with a cocktail stick; the front edge was folded back on itself to suggest forward movement, and various other adjustments were made to the lie of the fabric. As the putty began to stiffen it was possible to tease the rear edge upwards and outwards and to adjust the bottom of the folds to further enliven the flow of the drapery.

The remaining separate quarters of the caparison were similarly modelled and then left to harden; thus the basic shape of the drapery was established, and it really only remained to refine the roughness of the initial modelling with files and scrapers. There is no need to refine the caparison to scale thickness, as this would simply result in a flimsy structure without improving the appearance of the model.

ALTERATIONS TO THE KNIGHT

I intended Warwick to carry a standard, so his right arm needed to be repositioned to hold this aloft, preferably without having to alter the shape of the armoured part.

I first cut the sleeve of the surcoat away from the main body casting at the shoulder, then drilled a locating hole for the length of annealed brass rod on which I had mounted the right arm. This rod was cut so that when pushed into its locating hole the elbow and tips of the fingers were in the right positions relative to the shoulder; it was useful to refer to the drawing of human proportions in Chapter 1 at this stage. The arm was then twisted and bent on its soft brass rod into a position where, holding a quickly mocked-up banner, it looked right. The sleeve of the surcoat was built up from Milliput, and as it hardened a blunt needle was wetted and used to model the folds. Surcoats at this time seem to have been made from quite heavy material to which the heraldry was appliquéd, so it was modelled with rather ponderous folds to suggest this.

ABOVE The component parts are roughly assembled so that the fit and the appearance of the final model can be assessed at an early enough stage for minor revisions without too much agony. Work on the knight is still at an early stage, and the standard is still only roughly sketched.

To form a support for the Milliput I used Plastilene; I keep a stock of this product handy, because it doesn't stick fast to other materials and generally peels off cleanly in one piece. I warmed a quantity of this in the oven, and pressed it into a flat shape; then pushed part of the horse's neck into this. The flat side of the horse half was supported on but not pushed into this block. I then built up the shape of the inside of the caparison with Plastilene - this would be both a former and a support for the Milliput caparison. The other horse half was treated the same way; the preparation was now finished and the modelling work could begin.

I thought that if the knight's visor was raised he would make a more lively figure, and there was no reason for it to be down in this castle setting. Only the bevor that protected the lower part of the face and covered the upper part of the surcoat was integral to the main body casting, and this was cut away. I was sure that Warwick could safely dispense with this item, as in reality it must have been constricting and stuffy to wear when no action was likely. (In fact its absence was not unusual, even in battle: the son of Charles the Bold of Burgundy was killed in 1452 by a pike thrust when he wore the sallet without the bevor, and Charles himself was badly wounded by a

sword cut when his casually-attached bevor fell off in action.)

Removing the bevor from the model left the top of the cuirass and the round neck of the surcoat to be restated with Milliput, and this confronted me with the problem of the head. Although there are portraits of many prominent late 15th century personalities, no likeness of Richard Neville has survived. Other portraits of this time show that facial hair was unfashionable, so I bore this in mind when selecting a head with an open-faced sallet from my box of bits. After glueing it in place I detailed the visor. The 'sight' was opened with a fine drill and sharp scalpel; and

ABOVE The Essex knight Sir Thomas Montgomery of Folkborne at the hard-fought battle of Towton, 1461, where he was knighted by Edward IV. David Lane made the model from the same Border Miniatures kit that provided the starting point for my model of the Earl of Warwick.

RIGHT The monumental brass of Sir William Stapleton at Edenhall in Cumbria, dating from 1458. The open-visored sallet and short-sleeved heraldic surcoat were features which I included in my model of Neville. The heraldry alternates round the surcoat and sleeves, so that a back view would reveal the position of the rings and swords reversed. The Stapleton brass is one of the better examples of this type of monument in England. The artistic quality of monumental brasses was in decline in the second half of the 15th century, and caution should be exercised when interpreting these sources. In this case, although the armour is otherwise well drawn, the artist has forgotten to add the articulating lames of the leg armour above the knees. Sir William's plain little wife stands beside him on the monumental slab; I suspect that her size reflects her relative importance rather than her stature. I have included her in this drawing as a reminder of the possibilities presented by medieval ladies as modelling subjects. (Author's drawing)

after a lot of fiddling about - this was one of those jobs that needed three hands - I managed to solder the small, slippery item in place with only minor burns to the fingers. (I know that there are devices that offer to provide modellers with that 'third hand' which would be so useful in situations like this, but I've never got round to buying one. I usually manage to improvise my way out of these tricky positions with bits of Plastilene or whatever else is to hand.)

I added a mail collar from Milliput; then completed the head by refining the facial features, and adding a chinstrap from the same material. I considered adding a crest to the helmet, but the visored sallet doesn't afford this opportunity.

THE KINGMAKER'S HERALDRY

Richard Neville the elder, the 'Kingmaker's' father, was a younger son of Ralph, Earl of Westmorland. He married the heiress of Thomas Montagu and became Earl of Salisbury. His paternal arms were 'Gules, a saltire argent', which as a cadet he differenced with a 'label compony argent and azure'. He took the Lancastrian colours of silver and blue for the label because his mother was a daughter of John of Gaunt, Duke of Lancaster.

Salisbury's son, the 'Kingmaker', married the heiress of Richard Beauchamp to become Earl of Warwick. When his father was beheaded after the battle of Wakefield in 1460 he became Earl of Salisbury as well as Earl of Warwick, though he continued to style himself with the latter title. The crests of these earldoms are illustrated opposite.

Neville would have displayed on the front, back and short sleeves of his surcoat, and in four positions on his horse caparison, his personal coat-of-arms differenced from the paternal arms of Neville (while his father was still alive) with a silver and blue label.

Although the heraldry was simple, the saltire and 'label compony' had to be drawn accurately - and drawn eight times, too. Apart from this rather daunting prospect there were none of the design problems that can occur

RIGHT This view shows how the arm is attached to the shoulder by a brass rod on which it articulates to allow adjustments to be made to its position.

FAR RIGHT The hand and arm have been adjusted to hold the brass shaft of the standard which flows behind the figure. The surcoat sleeve has been modelled in Milliput and completes the arm assembly.

when painting heraldry on a three-dimensional item such as a surcoat or caparison. Painting the surcoat was the most difficult part, and there is no easy formula. By the time I started work on the horse's caparison I had evolved a system which speeded up the work, but still involved redefining the initial drawing several times. (See pp. 94 & 97.)

First I drew the label in blue, then added the outline of the saltire in red. Next I filled in the blue squares on the label, followed by the white squares between these, and then filled in the outline of the saltire. Then I painted the red background, which helped tidy up the outlines. This cycle was repeated three times, each time tightening up the work until an acceptable finish was achieved. The paint was applied quite thinly so it took at least three coats to cover, and the red proved particularly difficult in this respect. Only a minimum amount of shading was then

LEFT Coats-of-arms and crests: Richard Beauchamp, Earl of Warwick - a white swan's head and neck. Richard Neville, Earl of Salisbury - a demi-griffon. (Author's drawing from the Armorial de Gelre)

RIGHT The bowman on the wall. I had to remove some unwanted detail below the waist and refashion the area with modelling putty. At this stage I repositioned the arms so that the bow, arrow and bowstring would 'work' together. The bowstring will be added at the very last minute from waxed thread. Note that the archer has prudently taken a jug on duty with him.

LEFT The longbowman stares purposefully into the distance. I decided that the original sword 'didn't work', so I replaced it on his left hip with a short, heavy dagger. The sallet is cut away on the right hand side to enable the bowstring to be drawn to the cheek or ear. A short military flail lies on the wallwalk behind him, ready to repel scaling parties who get within hand-to-hand range.

added to the heraldry and caparison to accentuate the relief.

I painted the lining of the caparison green to complement the predominant red of the heraldry, and this worked well. Reference to my copy of *A European Armorial* suggested that a green lining was appropriate, as several of the knights illustrated used a comparable colour scheme. The colour of Warwick's horse needed some thought, as I wanted to retain a strong contrasting colour scheme overall.

LEFT I used a muted colour scheme accented only by the red hose and a glint of steel from the burnished armour. My bundled arrows again add an authentic detail to the threatening pose. Art lovers will recognise the landscape background as 'The Mill', a watercolour of 1494 by Albrecht Dürer. The paintings of Pieter Bruegel provide another rich source of late medieval backgrounds.

There was really little choice: the colour scheme demanded a grey, which afforded the best contrast to the dominant red and white heraldry. Warwick's grey is perhaps an authentic note, too; there are other instances of striking white horses belonging to great medieval leaders. At Agincourt a chronicler noted that Henry V had with him a *'magnifique destrier blanc comme la neige'*. It would seem appropriate to allow the great Earl of Warwick a similar flamboyant gesture.

THE BOWMAN ON THE WALL

I took as my starting point a kit sculpted by Rendal Patton for I & E Miniatures. I first dispensed with his effete Italianate bow and quiver - quite unsuitable for a late 15th century English longbowman. The essential problem when assembling a bowman, as we noted in Chapter 4, is to ensure that the arrow passes over the bow at right angles to it and meets the centre of the bowstring, which in turn should be taut. It sounds simple, but to

RIGHT A well-equipped billman with a visored sallet, padded jack and a murderous-looking polearm. He is also armed with a 'bollock dagger' and a heavy, curved falchion; and to judge by his haversack his duties will keep him out of reach of the castle kitchens all day. Built and painted by the author from an 80mm Border Miniatures kit.

RIGHT AND OPPOSITE The billman and a crossbowman of the castle garrison with their dog, photogaphed in different gateways. The figures don't really lend themselves to radical conversion work, so I built and painted them 'straight from the box'. They serve to bring incident and life to the model castle, and to illustrate the dress and equipment of the time. Weapons, stakes and tools leant against the wall also make an architectural setting look 'lived in'; and yes, I'm afraid it's that cat again - supremely unimpressed by the earl's retinue of two men and a dog...

ABOVE The arms of the Cumbrian knight Sir Lancelot de Threlkeld are displayed on his shield and lance pennon in this group. He was a personal retainer of the Earl of Warwick, and fought at the battle of Towton in 1461 on the Yorkist side. The helmet seen here is an 'armet' with an additional wrapper; articulated gorget plates reinforce the vulnerable throat area. A war hammer leans against the shield, which is of the shape associated with tournament jousting.

achieve this took a good deal of fiddling and repositioning of arms, hands and bow - not quite a conversion, but nearly. When the figure looked right I added a brass locating rod under the back foot so that he could stand alert on the wallhead eyeing the activity below.

I thought that the face might benefit from a little more character, and an instant trick for achieving this effect is to add a moustache. Facial hair was not in vogue amongst the upper ranks of society at this time, judging from contemporary portraiture; but I shouldn't think that archers always aped their betters in this respect. Incidentally, if you are having problems when working on a face and a moustache doesn't solve the problem, try a beard too. With a Scottish subject you may be able to get away with a large bushy one that covers half the face. If that doesn't work then you've got a bigger problem than you thought, so start again.

LIVERY BADGES & COLOURS

Badges were the distinctive sign worn by the retainers, servants and dependants of a knight or lord; they were used to indicate the ownership of goods and the allegiance of men. A knight's retinue would adopt his badge and livery colours, not his coat-of-arms, which was personal to him. Troops in the service of a great lord would display his livery colours and badge widely, so they became far better known and recognised than his coat-of-arms.

Perhaps the earliest example of a badge in use is the sprig of broom (Latin, *planta genista*) used by the Plantagenets, from which their name derived. The white boar badge of Richard III is well known, as are the blue boar of the Earls of Oxford, the ragged staff of Warwick, the white hart's head of Stanley, and several others. A later, universally recognised badge is the Tudor Rose, combining the white and red roses of the previously warring factions of York and Lancaster.

OVERLEAF The geometric heraldry has been drawn to size and positioned accurately, even if untidily at this stage. (Incidentally, remember that animate charges such as lions, in fact anything which might face in a particular direction, will always face towards the horse's head on both sides of a caparison.)

BANNERS & STANDARDS

Banners were square flags (though early examples were rather longer than they were broad) which carried the coat of arms of a knight or lord; they were a statement of the lands and titles that he held. Most were about 3ft 6ins square (106cm), though the greater lords may have displayed larger ones perhaps up to 5ft (152cm) square. Medieval flags were often stiffened, and some had a batten at least part way along the top edge to keep them always 'on the fly'.

A simpler flag for purposes of identification was the long livery flag known as a standard, which announced the owner's presence in person on the battlefield. In the hoist was displayed a national cross or device. The field or 'fly' was of the owner's livery colours, on which his various badges and motto appeared. These often bore no relation to the arms on the

knight's banner. Another simpler type of standard is also known; this was a square flag carrying a single device or badge on a coloured field.

TOP LEFT The banner of Richard Neville, Earl of Warwick, that 'overmighty subject'. This glorious mass of imagery is best deciphered in a leisurely manner. Richard Neville's personal arms appear in the third quarter, and are the arms he would have worn to identify himself in battle - not, as modellers will be relieved to hear, the entire design. The first quarter displays the arms of the Earldom of Warwick, the second those of Salisbury, and in the fourth are the quartered arms of Clare and Despenser.

CENTRE LEFT
(Top) Standard of Henry Percy, Earl of Northumberland. The Cross of St George is displayed in the hoist, and the badges and motto of the Percys on the red-over-black livery colours of the fly. (Bottom) Standard of the Scottish Douglas family, known as 'The Cavers Ensign'. The Cross of St Andrew is in the hoist and various Douglas badges are displayed on the fly. On the reverse of the standard the lion would face the staff, but the motto 'Jamais Arriere' would read right to left. It is thought that the standard originally had a forked tail.

BOTTOM LEFT Warwick's badges were first drawn onto the red background of his standard with thin white paint. The flag is made from pewter sheet; both sides were painted before the folds were pushed into place. There should be no problem with cracking of the paint surface - most paints (and particularly acryllics) are quite flexible, and will not crack even when the folds are quite tight. Obviously, experiment first with scraps of pewter and various paints - you don't want to find out the tolerance of your materials the hard way, after spending hours painting some gorgeously complex design.

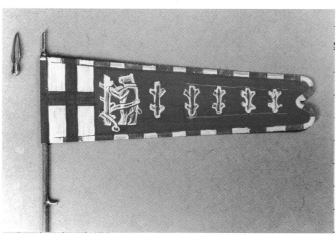

NON-MILITARY FIGURES IN MEDIEVAL SETTINGS

Figure modelling is essentially military figure modelling, so I was not surprised at the difficulty I encountered when I looked for commercially available non-military castings from the ancient and medieval worlds. I would have liked to include a medieval lady in my castle scene in Chapter 6, but in the scale in which I was working I could only find 'glamour' figures from the Phoenix range. Although these are very attractive and often amusing figures, I sadly decided that I couldn't find room for a 'Guinevere with chastity belt' in the scene I had in mind.

Most commercially available female figures fall into the mildly erotic category (sometimes even with a hint of bondage), and many cross the thin divide into the realm of fantasy. I'm sure that there is no shortage of subject matter to tempt modellers to try including non-military figures. After all, in ancient and medieval times there was really no such thing as a 'military' world wholly separate from civil society, and the two interacted all the time. The problem clearly lies in the lack of figure castings and kits which might provide a viable starting point.

RIGHT Andy Belsey and Adrian Bay collaborated to produce this extraordinary model of 'Brother Cadfael' at work in his herbarium surrounded by jars, jugs, pots, and pestles of every shape and size. Adrian made the inquisitive Benedictine by sculpting a new head and arm for the Andrea model of Sean Connery in the character of the worldly-wise Franciscan investigator in *The Name of the Rose*. As an architectural modelmaker Andy has a scrapbox well stocked with domestic containers from a variety of sources which he uses as props in his everyday work. These certainly came in handy for this project; I'm sure I can count at least 50 of them here.

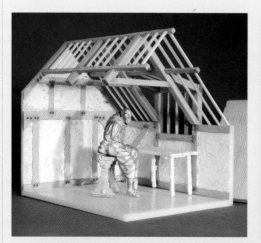 

LEFT A travelling tinker with his donkey tempts a medieval lady with his wares. (Model by Alice Armstrong from 54mm kits by Globe Figures)

LEFT 'Stitching the Standard': Geoff Illsley's demure medieval lady contrasts sharply with the stark castle wall, while the standard sounds a military note. This is a 1:32 scale model after a Pre-Raphaelite painting by Edmund Blair Leighton. (Photo G.Illsley)

CHAPTER 7

ANGLO-SAXON ENGLAND

RIGHT The relative plainness of the costume of most Northern European warriors in the Dark Ages, and the apparent scarcity of body armour, oblige the modeller to focus on the helmet, shield and weapons in order to introduce eye-catching features. This is particularly true if working in the larger scales.

The end of Roman administration in Britannia and the withdrawal of most of the garrison at the beginning of the 5th century AD marked the beginning of what we call the Dark Ages. Germanic peoples, mainly Angles, Saxons and Jutes who were threatened by the movement of nomadic tribes from the East, crossed the North Sea at first as raiders and later to find a new home for their families. Over centuries of steady encroachment they pushed the once-Romanised Celtic Britons into the far west. The haphazard nature of the migration of these peoples, and the second wave of Danish migrants who followed them, led eventually to the establishment of a fragmented series of small kingdoms. In the 9th century these began to be welded together into the Kingdom of England under the impulse of Alfred's West Saxon dynasty.

THE PROJECT

The vehicle chosen as the basis for this project is a 120mm commercial kit of a Viking warrior sculpted by the Swedish modeller Mike Blank

and produced in resin by Oakwood Studios. I had never worked in this large scale before, nor had I any experience of resin figures, which added interest to the project. My aim was to convert Mike's 9th century Viking

RIGHT The parts of Mike Blank's kit that I used as the basis of my model are shown here assembled with the aid of brass rods. The Viking's helmet has been cut away.

FAR RIGHT The new Milliput trousers are taking shape, the tunic has been lengthened, and the position of the left leg has been altered. The shield and spear are at a more advanced stage.

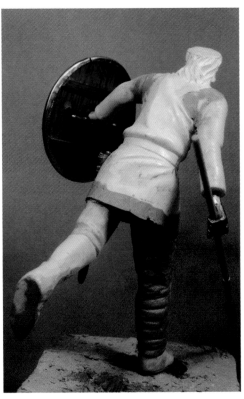

into a typical 7th century Anglo-Saxon warrior.

The style of the figure's tunic and trousers suit an Anglo-Saxon as well as a Viking - and, for that matter, probably most other Northern European peoples over a number of centuries. I did not intend to do any major conversion work on the figure itself, only to carry out minor modifications that would enable him to carry the new weapons and wear the helmet which I planned to fashion for him.

The construction in miniature of these authentic Anglo-Saxon weapons and armour based on archaeological and literary evidence form the core of this chapter. The methods described here can, of course, be applied to making weapons of any era, and readers should refer to them when tackling any projects suggested by earlier chapters.

Dark Age helmets and armour are exceedingly rare archaeological finds; however, I think it is arguable whether the rarity of armour - a precious possession - among grave goods reflects a similar scarcity on the battlefield. So, although my warrior is not of the highest rank, I decided to give him a helmet. This would lend itself to being made as far as possible from metal, and it would be an interesting little model in its own right. I decided that my warrior could do without a mail shirt, for which evidence is very rarely found in excavations of this period; he would have to rely on his shield for protection. Spears and shields are the most common finds in 5th and 6th century Anglo-Saxon burial grounds, followed by swords, seaxs, axes and arrows; I planned to make most of these and incorporate them into the model. When Christianity came to these islands weapons ceased to be deposited with burials, so we have to rely on chance finds to complete the later archaeological record.

ASSEMBLING THE RESIN FIGURE

Only an outline of this stage is needed, as the real interest of this project lies in the way in which the basic figure is modified.

I started by cutting the plain conical helmet away with a piercing saw and discarding it. Then I drilled quite deeply into the top of the legs, and glued brass locating rods in place. These, when inserted into the appropriately positioned holes in the body moulding, enabled me to position the legs precisely and at the same time to adjust the length. The arms were glued in place with super-glue, which formed a very quick and solid bond between the two resin surfaces. The hands were

mounted on locating rods, then drilled to take respectively the spear shaft and the shield grip. I wanted the spear to form a contrasting diagonal to the forward thrust of the figure, and the soft brass rod - now, in effect, the figure's wrist - allowed me to adjust this at will.

I positioned the assembled figure on a roughed-out piece of sloping groundwork. Even at this early stage it was beginning to work well from most viewpoints. I used Milliput as a filler and - fortunately, since I

ABOVE The shield board with its transverse struts in place; the turned brass shield boss is ready to be riveted on. Note the pewter blanks for the sword, spearhead, axe and seax.

LEFT The shield with the handle riveted in place behind the central hole.

RIGHT The shield board with the boss riveted in place.

FAR RIGHT The boss has been removed from the shield board to allow the first half of the sheet pewter covering to be glued on. The thin pewter sheet is soft and malleable, and can be persuaded into shape in much the same manner as the original shield's hide covering.

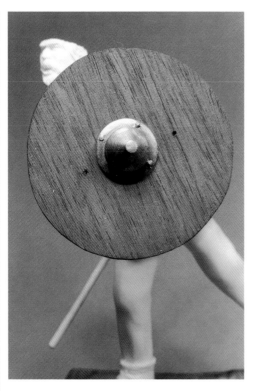

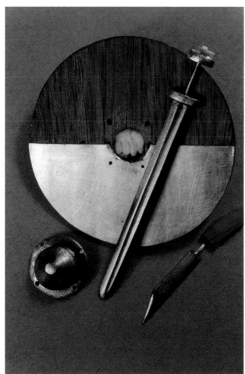

intended to use this to build on to the figure – I found that it adhered well to the resin. In lengthening the right leg and altering the angle of the left one I lost most of the original trousers, so I had to replace them with a new Milliput pair. It was only necessary to make the tunic a little longer before the figure was ready for the really interesting part of the exercise: modelling his weapons and equipment. However, it was difficult to resist adding a bit here and a bit there as the model progressed. In this way he acquired a pair of 'turnshoes' with ridged soles, fastenings and seams. Later I detailed the waist belt, made a decorative metal end for it, and modelled a leather bag to hang on the right hip. The amulet which swings outward on a thong round the warrior's neck was a finishing touch which added a feeling of movement to the composition.

THE ANGLO-SAXON SHIELD

I decided to make the shield from real scale wooden boards, and to construct it in much the same sequence as would have been followed by an Anglo-Saxon craftsman in the 6th century. The boards would only be visible from the rear of the shield as the front is covered with leather. I began by cutting the seven boards which made up the shield to length and gluing them edge to edge on a sheet of paper. I glued two struts the width of the shield at right angles to the boards, and

weighted the assembly down to ensure that it dried flat. These transverse pieces help to hold the boards in place, but are based on rather thin evidence.

The wooden boards do not survive in Anglo-Saxon burials, but their thickness can be deduced from the surviving metal rivets. The average thickness of the shield boards was only 7.5mm (5/16in), similar to Viking shields from the Continent; this makes the use of dowels to fit the boards together improbable. A glued butt-joint would provide little strength, and though a lap-joint is a possibility the use of horizontal members seems more probable. The diameter of Anglo-Saxon shields can be inferred from surviving metal fittings and other indicators, which show that the average width was about 2 feet (61cm). Although larger shields are found up to 3 feet (91.5cm) in diameter, many small ones are, surprisingly, only 12ins (30.5cm) across.

The thin wooden shield was easily damaged in combat, and this emerges clearly from the written sources. Modellers who like to include battle damage will find inspiration in the vivid description of a shield after a battle in the Welsh poem *Y Gododdin* – 'There did not come back of it as much as a hand could grip'. The Vikings, presumably for this reason, allowed the combatants in a duel the use of up to three shields in turn.

The iron shield boss was about 7ins (17.8cm) across, and I made it from brass in three parts. A slim 14mm brass washer served

FAR LEFT The covering on the face of the shield is complete and the awkward edging strip has been persuaded into place round the outer rim. Note the profile of the boss; the decorative studs flanking it, and the rivets securing it, are now formed from steel dressmaking pins. Work on the new Milliput trousers is advancing, and the spearhead is approaching its final form.

LEFT The finished shield displays an iron boss, decorative studs and applied fish decoration. A bronze clip covers the gap where the ends of the rim binding meet; these clips are often found in Anglo-Saxon graves and are associated with the shield, but it is not certain that they were used in this manner.

as the flange, and I drilled four evenly spaced rivet holes around the edge. The 'wall and cone' section of the boss was turned from 10mm round section brass in my primitively contrived lathe. This was drilled to take the apex, which was formed from a crankpin from a 00 gauge loco wheel. Brass rod was inserted into the holes in the flange to act as rivets; then the completed assembly was soldered together with the torch. I cut a hole in the centre of the shield as a tight fit for the clenched fist which I drilled out to take the hand grip.

The iron handles were riveted in place through the shield, and most were quite short; long ones are sometimes found, however, and I chose to model one of these as it would be more visible. I annealed a short length of brass rod by heating and cooling; flattened the ends with a hammer; then drilled four holes to take the brass rivets which would secure it in place. Some work with a fine file on the flattened ends produced an approximation of the shape of the real iron handle. This assembly was then glued in place. With the help of my Mini-Drill I ground away enough brass from the inside of the shield boss to allow it to fit over the protruding fist.

Next I turned my attention to the leather covering of the shield board. I made this from sheet pewter, which I glued on to the wood in two halves to simulate the horizontal join between the two pieces of hide with which these shields were covered. The edging seems to have been leather too, and this was a

problem that took several attempts to solve. Eventually I realised that the best way was to cut a thin strip of pewter that would go right round the edge of the shield and overlap both sides. The strip was held on the edge of a steel ruler and pushed into a gutter shape which would fit over the shield rim. I held this on to the top of the shield with one hand and worked it gradually into place round the circumference with the other. No glue was used at this stage, but when I thought the edging looked convincing I removed it carefully and then glued it back securely in place.

After this the fitting of the boss was a simple matter; I glued it in place, then drilled through the shield using the four rivet holes as guides. I made the rivets from pins which I cut very short and glued in place so that the shanks protruded only a fraction through the back of the shield board. There remained only the decoration of the shield to consider.

SHIELD DECORATIONS

About half of the Anglo-Saxon shields discovered display some form of relief decoration. The most common is in the form of iron studs fastened through the shield in two pairs on either side of the boss. A few silvered or gilt bronze relief decorations have been found in the forms of either geometric lozenges or fish, birds and stylised quadrupeds. A small metal clip also turns up

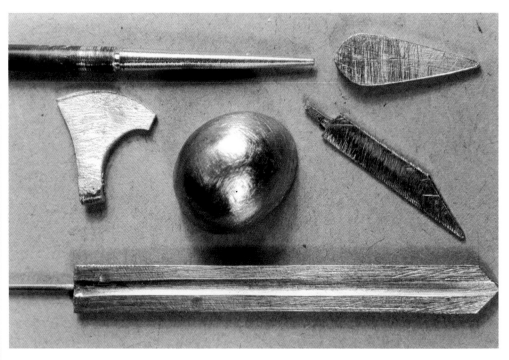

ABOVE The legendary hero 'Beowulf' was sculpted by Keith Durham armed in the manner of a 6th century Anglo-Saxon chieftain. The applied metal shield decorations are derived from artefacts excavated at Sutton Hoo and from illustrations in the Lindisfarne Gospels. Beowulf's splendid helmet is based on the Coppergate find. The model was painted by the author from one of his own kits.

ABOVE RIGHT The pewter blanks can be seen beginning to develop into miniature weapons. The leaf-shaped spearhead is roughed out and ready to be spliced to the turned brass shank. The shapes of the axe and seax are fully developed, as is the iron helmet bowl in the centre. The sword blank is still a flat rectangle, but a brass tang has been added and the fuller has been carefully filed in.

occasionally, which may have fitted over the shield rim to cover the join in the leather edging. There is some evidence to suggest that shields were often stained red, and that some may have displayed leather appliqué shapes.

MODELLING THE WEAPONS

The construction of the axe and seax can be followed in the captioned photographs. I have rather concentrated my detailed description here on the materials and methods which I used to make the sword and spear, as practically all other kinds of edged weapons are made in the same way.

Anglo-Saxon swords were neither big nor heavy; the archaeological evidence suggests that an average blade was about 2ft 3ins (71cm) long and weighed 1½ pounds (0.68 kilos). Blades were straight and two-edged, usually with a fuller running the whole length. Finished blades from a limited number of production centres were distributed throughout Europe; the hilts, however, were mounted locally, and these provide the evidence for their place of origin. The identification of a sword hilt as Anglo-Saxon, Danish or Frankish depends simply on the locality in which the majority of that particular type have come to light, and the same is true of other weapons.

I started work by casting some pewter blanks from simple shapes cut in the back of old silicone rubber moulds; these blanks would become the spearhead and the blades of the other weapons. Pewter is mainly tin and is a hard but malleable metal which can still be

carved readily with simple hand tools. It does not clog files and saws so readily as does white metal, and as it melts at a relatively high temperature it is easily soldered.

The sword blade entailed some precise work; as it was the difficult one I started work on it first. If I could make a good job of this, I thought, the others would seem simple. Anglo-Saxon swords had a groove or fuller running the length of the blade, and this presented the main problem. I first cleaned up the rough pewter blank in the workshop vice with a fairly coarse file until I had a more precise block with smooth surfaces. This was slightly wider and thicker than the blade that would ultimately emerge from it. Next, working under the magnifying lamp and using a craft knife against a steel rule, I marked the position of the 1.5mm parallel groove on both sides of the shiny pewter blank. I cut away the cast tang, which was in the way; then, working carefully inside the incised lines, I filed the groove the length of the blade on both sides of the block with a fairly coarse-cut round file.

I marked a centreline on the narrow edges of the block and, using this and the lines which marked the edge of the fuller as a guide, I bevelled the four edges of the blade. I had to hold the work in my fingers to do this, but fortunately the pewter was strong and showed no sign of bending. At the completion of this stage, though the bevels should be cut right up to the guidelines, these should still be visible. The blade was now given a taper by running a flat file along the edge, which made it necessary to restate the bevel, particularly

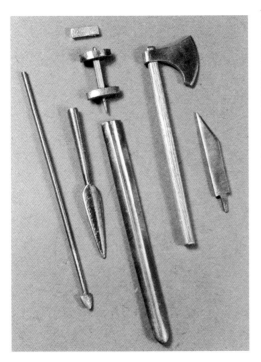

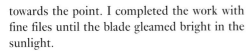

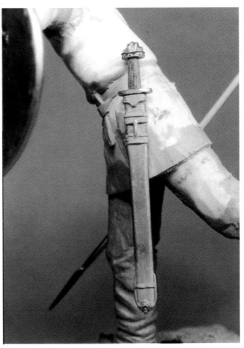

towards the point. I completed the work with fine files until the blade gleamed bright in the sunlight.

THE SWORD HILT

The hilt of an Anglo-Saxon sword consisted of a lower guard, grip, upper guard and pommel, all of which were pierced to fit in turn on to the tang of the blade.

I drilled the flat part of my blade nearest the hilt to take a length of brass rod which would form the tang. In a similar way a 6th century swordsmith would have spliced a tang into a hardened blade and welded it in place. I decided to make the grip from real wood, so I glued two lengths of fine-grained miniature planking face to face to produce the required thickness. This was then cut to length and drilled lengthways to fit the tang. Sword grips were oval and quite short, so that the hand fitted tight between the upper and lower guards.

I made the guards from pewter scraps which I held down with a fingernail while I cut and filed the metal to shape. This was a fiddly job, and the tiny metal ovals tended to flick off into space exasperatingly; I spent some time on my hands and knees during this stage of the project. The oval guards were drilled centrally; then a thin strip of pewter was soldered across the top of the upper one to form the basis of the pommel. The component parts of the hilt were now ready to assemble onto the tang, which would make them much easier to handle and finish. I soldered the blade to the lower guard; then slotted the wooden grip into position, and finally glued the upper guard and pommel onto the tang.

THE SPEAR

The spear was the main weapon of the Anglo-Saxon warrior. They were made of iron, and consisted of a blade of widely varying shape and a socket which was split so that it could be hammered to fit onto the wooden shaft. The leaf-shaped blade which I chose to model was a common form, but more exotic shapes can be made in exactly the same way.

I made the socket of the spear first, by filing a taper on a length of brass rod with the help of my Mini-Drill (this is explained in Chapter 1). This was parted off and the wider end was then drilled to take the wooden shaft. The leaf-shaped blade of the spear was sawn and filed from a pewter blank, then notched to take the brass socket. The brass and pewter parts were then soldered together. Most Anglo-Saxon spear blades were of diamond cross-section, so the pewter blade was worked with a series of files of increasingly fine cut to achieve this shape. I made the spear shaft from a cocktail stick, and riveted the metal socket to the shaft with a tiny brass pin.

THE HELMET PROBLEM

Before I could start work on the model helmet I had to decide on an appropriate style from the evidence available, and this is limited since only four Anglo-Saxon helmets have ever been

ABOVE FAR LEFT The weapons are here approaching their final form. The sword blade has now been bevelled, tapered and pointed with a series of fine files. The components of the hilt are displayed here mounted on the tang, which has been removed from the blade. The pommel at the top has not been filed to shape yet, but will locate on to the top of the tang which can be seen protruding through the oval upper hilt guard. The square brass grip was discarded in favour of a real wooden one at this stage. The axe head is mounted on its brass shaft, but the sides of the socket hole await the addition of the characteristic pointed projection which enables us to identify an Anglo-Saxon axe.

ABOVE CENTRE & RIGHT The details of the scabbard, its mounts and the manner in which the sword is suspended from the waist belt were suggested by a variety of sources mentioned in the Bibliography. I modelled the detail in Milliput on top of the sword supplied in the kit, and after deciding to display my scratch-built sword separately I modified this hilt and replaced the grip with one made from wood. It is not entirely clear how Anglo-Saxon swords were suspended, but my recon-struction leans heavily on recent interpretations of the finds from the Sutton Hoo burial.

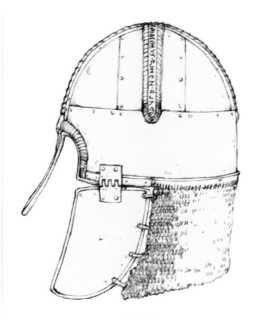

RIGHT The Coppergate helmet was found in York in 1982, and my drawing shows it after conservation work which revealed a practically intact helmet in a remarkable state of preservation.

FAR RIGHT The Benty Grange helmet is fragmentary and my drawing is a reconstruction of its probable appearance. Boar crests are associated with the pagan goddess Fryja and symbolise strength.

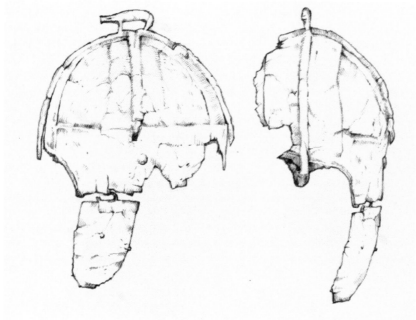

ABOVE Two drawings of the recently discovered Pioneer helmet. Although only four Anglo-Saxon helmets have been discovered, when we consider that only a single example of a Viking helmet has ever been unearthed this is riches indeed.

found. The earliest and most richly decorated of these is from the Sutton Hoo ship burial, which is thought to be that of the 7th century East Anglian King Raedwald who died in 625 AD; it is possible, however, that the helmet dates from the previous century. The 8th century helmet from Coppergate in York, and the recently discovered 'Pioneer' helmet possibly of 7th century origin, display striking constructional similarities. The Benty Grange helmet is of quite different construction, and has more in common with the *spangenhelm* which was in widespread use on the Continent in the 6th and 7th centuries. A few decorative fragments found in Dumfriesshire may be from the brow band of a helmet of this type, but there is no conclusive evidence that they were in use in Britain.

I couldn't equip my 'typical' Anglo-Saxon warrior with a king's helmet such as that from Sutton Hoo; nor would the richly decorated example from York have been appropriate. My warrior needed a simple helmet, and neither the Pioneer helmet (despite its lack of decoration) nor the crested Benty Grange helmet could be described as simple. I decided that a spangenhelm would probably be the most appropriate style to equip him with, despite there being only flimsy archaeological evidence for its use in Britain. Spangenhelms, possibly produced in northern Italy, have turned up in Germany and France, so it is probable that helmets of this type found their way to Britain too during this period of widespread migration.

MODELLING THE SPANGENHELM

Spangenhelms were constructed from four plates of iron (or occasionally other materials) which were held together by bronze bands or *spangen* to which they were riveted. Bronze cheek pieces were hinged to an iron brow band, which in at least some cases had a covering of thin metal foil covered with fine relief decoration. I decided to make the skull and cheek plates of the helmet from metal, as this would be quick and provide a strong, solid structure to build upon.

A rummage in my scrap box turned up a medieval sallet which, with the neck guard removed, became the bowl of my spangenhelm. I made the cheek pieces from thin pewter and soldered them in place. It was evident at this early stage that there was a distinct resemblance to the helmets of the Pioneer and Coppergate type. The brow band

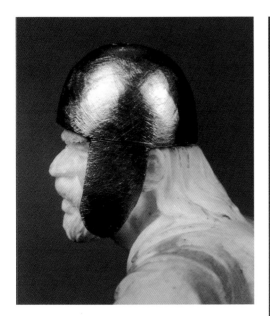

and its decoration were considered next. I recalled that Adrian Bay had recently described to me a method of suggesting subtle relief detail; it was simple and quick, so I tried it. I added the brow band from Milliput, and as this hardened I used a small round tool to impress random overlapping shapes until I had built up a pattern that seemed from a distance to be more than it really was.

The *spangen* were added by first covering the bowl of the helmet with a thin, smooth layer of epoxy putty. Then I cut through this to the metal, and removed the panels between the bands to leave them in relief. The positions of the rivets that held the iron segments together were then impressed into the hardening putty with a round tool. These circular impressions are usually quite adequate to represent rivets, but I thought that in this case the helmet would look better if domed rivet heads were added.

RIVET DETAIL

Adding rivet detail is repetitive and time-consuming, but adds a worthwhile finishing flourish to a model in this large scale. I tried three different ways of making domed rivet heads to see which was the quickest. I made a few from tiny balls of solder which I cut in half with a knife and glued in place. This gave a good result when everything went right - but it didn't often. Next I tried rolling tiny balls of modelling putty and sticking them on, which was much quicker. I transferred the minute shapes to the helmet with a brush and glued them on with a Milliput paste, which I made by working water into very freshly mixed Milliput with a stiff paintbrush. The

tiny balls need to be pressed into place and reshaped a little with the brush before being finished with another coat of thin paste. At this stage I realised that my spangenhelm - despite my reducing the number of rivets from those on helmets of which I had photographs - would need at least 50 rivets.

I asked Keith Durham how he made rivets; then I asked Rendal Patton the same question; but their replies were the same - 'One at a time, and slowly'. There was no quicker way, so I set to, and by the end of an hour I had most of the 50 in place and was becoming quite a slick hand at the job.

The rivets on the pewter cheek pieces were made in a different way. First I impressed tiny circles into the metal to mark the position of the rivets. Then I put a knob of flux inside each circle, and picked up a minute blob of very low-melt solder with the iron, which I transferred to the fluxed area to form the rivet head. This was a successful method and surprisingly quick, the solder invariably forming a rivet head within the impressed

ABOVE LEFT The cheek pieces have been soldered to the metal bowl of the spangenhelm to form the basic shape on to which the rest of the detail can be modelled.

ABOVE The metal parts of the helmet have been refined and the bronze browband has been added in Milliput. A simple random pattern has been impressed into this, which when painted should seem to be more than it really is. At this stage the rivet positions are marked but they have not yet been added in relief.

RIGHT You can see what the component parts of the helmet have been made from in this close-up of the completed modelling work. The diamond-shaped metal segments between the *spangen* will now be burnished to represent iron plates. The rest of the helmet is bronze and will have to be painted, as will the mail neck guard which has been added from Milliput. An amulet swinging on a thong round the neck serves to add movement to the figure.

RIGHT The completed spangenhelm; it is at this stage that the relief decoration on the brow band works most effectively. Note the rivets on the back of the shield; the inner ones hold the boss in place, the outer ones are the decorative studs.

circle; however, the limitation of this method is that it can only be used to form a rivet on a metal surface.

This brought the construction of the spangenhelm near completion; I added a chinstrap, and topped the helmet off with a brass plume-holder made from part of a watch strap that I found in my scrap box. I finished the helmet by first buffing the iron skull pieces to a bright shine, then varnishing them. Then I painted the bronze parts, using a dry-brushing technique and working from dark to light. I used gold enamel for this, to which I added a touch of red for a bronze effect and a little black to darken it. When it was dry the completed spangenhelm was given its final sheen with two thin coats of varnish.

DISPLAYING THE WEAPONS

It occurred to me that the sword I had spent so much time making would be difficult to use with the Anglo-Saxon warrior. I couldn't fit it into his hand easily, so that only left the option of including it amongst the groundwork. I thought it deserved better than this; so I decided to make a separate setting to display the weapons. I modified the hilt of the sword which came with the kit, upon which I built up the slung scabbard. I cast a second spear, and made a second, sheathed seax for the warrior's belt.

The display of unsheathed weapons would need to be propped up against something – a structure of some sort, or a tree or rock. Well, there are plenty of rocks about the Lake District; but I thought that an appropriate and atmospheric setting might be achieved by fashioning a Neolithic standing stone or part of a stone circle. Perhaps our warrior had paused awhile to rest by the stones, which would have been ancient even in his day, their magical purpose shrouded in superstition and obscured by the passage of centuries. Not much more than a mile from our house in an elevated position, surrounded by the mountains of Northern Lakeland, stands 'The Carles', one of the most impressive late Neolithic great circles in Britain. I set out one sunny morning and made my way up to the prehistoric site, where I took a series of photos that would provide the reference I needed to build the model I had in mind. You might well ask, 'Why didn't he just use a real stone out of the beck?' I did consider this, but decided that the best way to achieve the quality of a venerable, weathered standing stone in miniature was to make one. You can judge the success of this for yourselves from the accompanying photographs.

FINISHING TOUCHES

It was time for the final painting. First I turned my attention to the shield, which I painted red since there was some evidence for this, and I thought that it worked well with the iron boss and the other decoration. As to the colour of the rest of the clothing, I had nothing to go on; so I turned to a particularly well-produced book of photos of recreated Vikings (see Nurmann, Schulze & Verhülsdonk in Bibliography). This provided a wealth of convincing reconstructions of Dark Age clothing and suggested some interesting colour schemes.

Although it covers a subject some 200–300 years later than my warrior, there was certainly

ABOVE The model is complete to the last detail and ready to undercoat; the grey areas of Milliput show the additions and alterations to the figure.

LEFT I added a leather wallet and a sheathed seax to the warrior's right hip to balance the composition.

RIGHT The initial set-up of the groundwork for the standing stone; some undulations are modelled with card on the plywood base. A particular stone from the circle has been drawn to scale, then cut out as a flat shape and positioned.

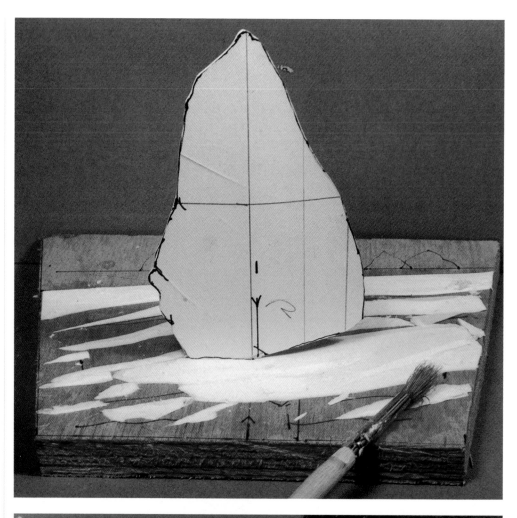

RIGHT I worked from my photographs and drawings and sculpted the shape of the stone quickly but accurately in modelling putty onto the card former. A second card profile, taken at right angles to the first, helped with the modelling and can still be seen protruding through the putty in the centre of the stone.

a strong similarity of material culture among the Northern European peoples of the Dark Ages, particularly in terms of fabrics, dyes, and general cut. (Indeed, even pre-Christian era burials in northern Germany and Denmark have been found to wear the 'classic' thigh-length tunic and loose trousers, so a 7th century subject presented no problems of conscience.) The colour plates were strong on female attire, too, and there were several that presented some very tempting subjects for future modelling projects. The book was a mine of fascinating Viking artefacts, and I couldn't resist adding a few to my Anglo-Saxon warrior, who owes his shoes, belt finial and leather pouch to this source, as well as his colour scheme.

The figure is sculpted in a fairly broad style so I adopted a similar manner when I painted it and, though I shaded the clothing, I didn't try to paint in subtleties of detail that didn't exist. Finally, though I resisted the lure of a checkered pattern on the trousers, I painted a red edging to the tunic which helped to bring the rather dull green of the garment to life. Contrasting edging was probably the most common of all garment decoration at this time, though I also resisted the multi-coloured tablet-woven braid which seems to have been particularly associated with Scandinavian clothing.

The wooden base had become rather untidy as I built up the groundwork, and needed facing. I had some scraps of veneer handy that came from a local cabinetmaker's workshop, and these proved ideal for the job. I glued the veneer in place, then cut it to shape and finished it with sandpaper and varnish.

LEFT How the weapons and the landscape setting were photographed.

ABOVE You can see what materials the model was made from in this view of the completed setting. Grass mat now covers most of the base, but sections have been cut away to add areas of interest which also lead the eye into the picture. Behind the rim of the shield you can see a puddle of water which I added from pewter sheet. In the background is the photograph which I used to produce the two backdrops employed behind the finished model.

OVERLEAF The dramatic presence of the time-ravaged monolith under a threatening sky adds an almost surreal atmosphere to the landscape in which the weapons are displayed.

PAGE 113 'Anglo-Saxon warrior, 7th century AD'.

CHAPTER 8

THE ROMAN ARMY IN NORTH BRITAIN

ABOVE The shield design and remodelled mail shirt are well displayed in this view of the completed trooper and horse. The helmet, modelled for me by Rendal Patton, had an iron skull skinned with bronze and chased with simulated locks of hair - a common feature in the archaeological record. The actual colours of fabric items like the scarf, cloak and tunic are largely guesswork; the latest academic opinion is that most Roman soldiers would have worn tunics of unbleached off-white woollen cloth, and there is some evidence for the winter cloak being a yellowish brown.

I n the early 2nd century AD the Emperor Hadrian ordered the building of a wall across northern Britain from the river Tyne in the east to the Solway Firth in the west. Although intended as a means to control the tribes both in the occupied province of Britannia south of the wall and in the as-yet unoccupied zone north of it, in time the wall came to mark the northern frontier of the Roman Empire. The garrisons of the forts that were built at intervals a long the wall were normally provided by auxiliary units from other parts of the empire rather than by the heavy infantry of the citizen Legions, which were stationed at strategic fortresses well inside Britannia. The garrisons of the northern marches included several cavalry regiments or *ala* ('wings').

THE PROJECT

We know from inscriptions found at Burgh-by-Sands and other sites that the *Ala I Tungrorum*, a regiment roughly 500 strong which recruited among the Tungri of Gallia Belgica (Belgium), served on Hadrian's Wall in the 2nd century. A trooper of this auxiliary unit, standing with his mount with the wall as a background, forms the subject of the featured model in this section.

THE ROMAN CAVALRY HORSE

Archaeological evidence shows that, at a little over 14 hands on average, Roman cavalry mounts were somewhat smaller than their modern counterparts. They were of various breeds, and were selected for their stamina, spirit, agility, and build from the best stock of the Roman Empire. Cavalry horses depicted in surviving relief sculpture are not carved in proportion to their riders, so we gain no impression of their true size; however, there is no mistaking that the horses were well-formed and spirited beasts.

The horse that I took as my starting point was from an 80mm medieval kit; the pose was just what I needed and the conformation seemed right for a Roman cavalry mount, though it would require the modelling of more

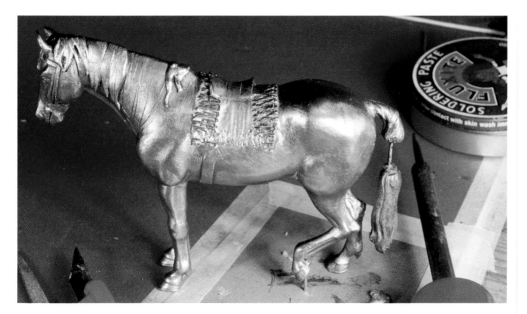

TOP LEFT At this early stage the unwanted medieval harness detail has been removed and I have begun to build up the locks of the mane with very low-melt solder. A brass supporting rod has been soldered into place below the raised hoof, and I have started work on the tail. Note also the simple soldering equipment and tools that I use.

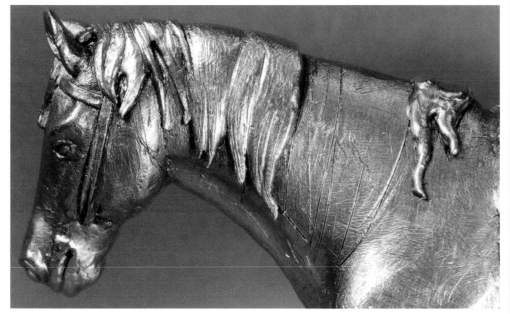

CENTRE LEFT In this close-up of the mane you can see the amount of control that can be achieved when working with very low-melt solder. Some work has been done with files to shape and refine the locks nearest the horse's head.

BOTTOM LEFT Modelling work on the mane is now at an advanced stage, and the bridle is beginning to take shape.

RIGHT The Roman saddle under construction; the horns have been pegged in place with short lengths of brass rod. Peter Connolly's books - see Bibliography - provide clear reference for this part of the model.

RIGHT In this view you can see work progressing on the saddle; the decorative breast band is in place, and the straps of the harness are being added. On the red card beside the *spatha* hilt are the patterns from which the harness roundels and the pendant crescents will be cast.

mane and tail and probably some 'feather' around the hooves.

The horse looked too big when matched with an 80mm figure, but when I stood a 90mm figure beside it they made a much better pair. The 80mm kit horse measured 77mm to the withers. Taking the linear scale of a 90mm figure to be 1ft = 15mm, this meant that the horse stood 5ft 1in or 15 hands, so it was about right. I soldered the components of the horse kit together, then carved away the unwanted medieval horse furniture and removed the stylised mane.

The reference sources I had for my horse were illustrations by Ron Embleton and Peter Connolly, along with some photos of a particularly convincing re-enactment unit with its mounts in Dan Peterson's book (see Bibliography). In addition to the horse these sources illustrated in great detail both the Roman style saddle and a variety of decorated horse furniture.

I wanted to model the horse with a long mane and tail in a naturalistic manner, so I began by looking closely at the ways in which the mane fell in a variety of pictorial sources before starting modelling. I drew the mane on to the casting first with a knife point, thinking in terms of locks of hair so as to give it movement and variety but without it becoming too stylised. I built up the locks of the mane working from the head down the length of the neck, using very low-melt solder rather than Milliput as I thought it would be the faster method. This type of solder is a surprisingly plastic medium when handled properly; it can be applied in a series of blobs which fuse into each other to build up shape, or can be made to trail into linear forms and teased into points - it is in fact ideal for this type of work. As it sets immediately you can

work on both sides of the horse at the same time without risking putting your fingers into still-wet Milliput detail on the other side. I smoothed the locks of the mane with files and scrapers next, taking care that the shapes retained a lively, fluid feeling. A suggestion of hair was added finally with the side of a flat file which I pulled down the locks in a firm, controlled movement, following the flow of the mane.

The horse's tail needed to be lengthened, so I first soldered it in place, then sawed off the bottom. I then reconnected this to the top part with a length of brass wire. This made a solid structure on which to model the missing section, which was built up with solder and textured in a similar manner to the mane.

THE SADDLE, HARNESS & DECORATION

I built up most of the bridle with solder, and made the rings which attach the reins to the snaffle bit from soft brass wire. The rest of the harness and saddlery were modelled from Milliput. I added the saddle blanket first, then modelled the rough shape of the saddle and its girth.

I was confused at this point, because many depictions of Roman cavalry horses show a longer, decorative saddle cloth, and suggest that the girth is underneath this. In this case the blanket must have either gone over the saddle itself or had a hole cut for the girth to pass through. (This latter solution would have kept the girth fastening buckles out of the way of the rider's legs nicely, but this thought did not occur to me until after I had modelled the girth over the blanket.) On balance, the sculptures would seem to suggest that there were two items: there must always have been a conventional blanket to provide a pad under the saddle, and in some cases a larger cloth seems to have been thrown over the saddle, for comfort or display.

I made the horns of the saddle from cylinders of Milliput which I drilled through, then fitted on to brass locating rods which I positioned at the corners of the saddle. These were further refined by filing and adding scraps of putty as the model progressed. I turned next to a photo of the well-known late 1st century tombstone of Titus Flavius Bassus, which provided a first hand source of information. From this I took the harness roundels and crescent pendants, and the fringed breast band, which I thought would make a

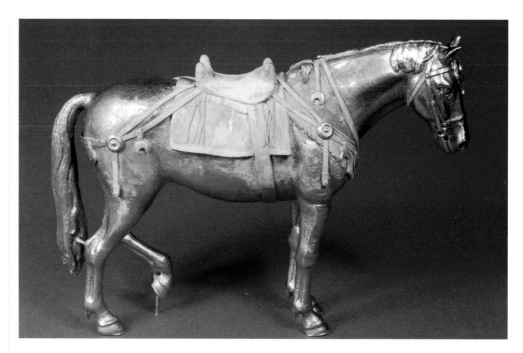

RIGHT AND BELOW RIGHT
You can see which parts have been made from low-melt solder and which from Milliput in these views of the finished horse. I needed ten castings of the pendant crescents and five discs to complete the decoration of the harness.

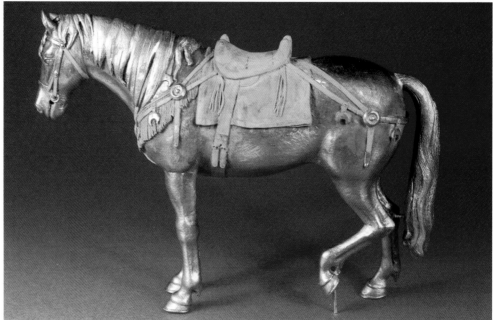

colourful addition to the model. I made the decorative breast band by modelling the shape on to the horse in Milliput, then impressing the fringes into this with a knife blade.

The roundels presented more of a problem; a solution would have been to turn them on a lathe, but I lack the equipment for this kind of work. I needed five roundels and at least ten crescents, so I thought it would be worthwhile in this case to make a mould and cast as many as I needed. I made the pattern for the crescent from Milliput by using circular cutters - in much the same way as biscuits are cut out - to produce the tiny shape. (Old paint brush ferrules are useful for this kind of work - they make ideal tools for cutting and impressing

round shapes.) This was modelled on a piece of card for ease of handling; then, after it had hardened, it was cut off its backing. A small brass axle bush from a model railway kit formed the basis of the roundel; I glued it to a card backing and filed it down to produce the low profile I wanted. I added Milliput to this shape and formed the central boss with a hollow tool pressed into the soft putty.

I won't bother you with the business of making silicone rubber moulds here, but if you want details of the process then the firm of Alec Tiranti produce a technical booklet on the subject and supply the materials needed - see Appendix A. (It is also well covered - along with some interesting information on Roman

building techniques, incidentally - in *Roy Porter's Model Buildings Masterclass* in this book series.) My mould produced a set of cast roundels and crescents which I glued in place on and under the strapwork of the breast band and crupper. The hangers for the crescents were added later, as were the thongs which hang from the saddle to attach the trooper's gear. Apart from a good deal of tidying up this completed the detailing of the horse.

THE AUXILIARY CAVALRYMAN

I knew of no 90mm auxiliary cavalryman in any manufacturer's list, so I looked for a figure that was as near to what I wanted as possible. The Italian firm Decima provided this in the form of a 1st century auxiliary infantryman. He was the right size and was posed in the right position, so I hoped that it wouldn't be too big a job to convert him into a cavalry trooper. I intended the figure to stand beside the horse holding the reins in his right hand, which would need to be repositioned slightly.

I wanted my cavalryman to have a decorated helmet like that of Titus Flavius Bassus, as there is archaeological evidence that these were worn by troops stationed in Northern Britain. This presented a problem, as the head in the kit would have to be substantially remodelled and I wasn't sure that I had the time to do it. I showed the head to Rendal Patton, who I knew was good at Roman helmets. He said that it would be quicker to start from scratch and make a completely different head than to spend time trying to alter it. I had suspected this from the onset so, as he seemed keen to do the work and I knew he was quick, I left it with him. This arrangement allowed me to concentrate my effort on the horse and gave me time to consider a realistic setting for the pair. I needed a day out, so I decided to do some field work.

A TRIP TO VINDOLANDA

The best surviving sections of Hadrian's Wall are only an hour away from my home, so I drove up there early one sunny spring morning. Vindolanda was both a fort and a civilian settlement, sited a short distance south of the Roman Wall. There have been some important and astonishingly well-preserved discoveries here during the extensive and on-going excavation work by the Birley family. Like most Roman sites, what remains is a sort of relief ground-plan, though the walls of the fort stand in places to over 6ft high - taller than usual. There are two interesting reconstructions of short sections of Hadrian's Wall, one of the original turf and timber defence and one of the

RIGHT The wooden gateway through the turf wall at Vindolanda. I photographed the reconstructed sections of the Roman Wall at Vindolanda extensively, as they provided good source material for future modelling projects. The turf and timber rampart section has deliberately been allowed to degrade over the years, so that historians can estimate how long such defences lasted without repair.

later stone wall that replaced it. Neither of them looked as if the Roman Army had a hand in their construction; nevertheless they were the material I needed, so I photographed them from all angles. I noticed that the section of turf wall had developed a pronounced droop in places, and wondered if this was due to the lack of a firm foundation. I wasn't sure whether the Romans had built their turf wall on a stone base, but I knew that the later Antonine Wall in Scotland was constructed on a massive stone foundation.

A ROMAN CAVALRY SHIELD

Once back at my work table, I decided to model a hexagonal shield based on one carried by a cavalryman on a sculptured panel from Trajan's Column in Rome. He is usually identified as a trooper of an élite Praetorian Guard unit, which is unlikely to have served in Britain (except, perhaps, during the Emperor Hadrian's visit in 122 AD?) Nevertheless this shape of shield, which is associated with Germanic tribes and is seen on other cavalry tombstones, may well have been favoured by

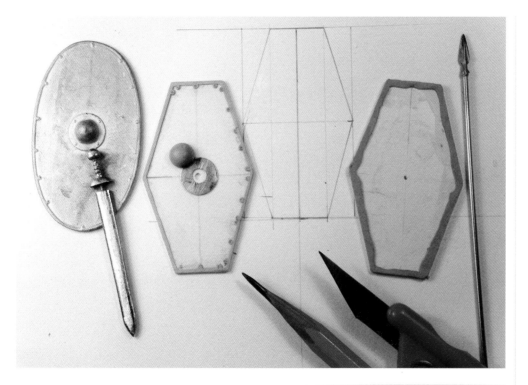

LEFT You can see here the progressive stages in the construction of the hexagonal shield, from the initial drawing through to the detailing of the boss and edging. On the left, resting on the shield from the kit, is the *spatha*; the hilt is ready to locate by means of a brass rod on to the new longer scabbard. This will then be finished by modelling the chape and suspension mounts.

the troopers of the *Ala I Tungrorum*.

I took the height of the straight-sided shield from the oval one in the kit which it was replacing. With this dimension as a starting point I began by drawing the shield on paper to help get the proportions right. Auxiliary shields were flat, so using the drawing as a guide I cut the shape out from a sheet of 1/16in plasticard.

The most difficult part of making Roman shields is finding a way to reproduce the fine brass binding which was riveted round the edge. I considered incising the edging into the plasticard, but eventually I decided to add it from modelling putty, which enabled me to make a convincing job of the rivets that held it in place. The shield boss was made from a conveniently sized brass washer which I filed down to a finer profile, along with a ball of Milliput which I cut in half to form the dome. The edging on the back of the shield had to be made in a similar manner; then the stiffening bars were added, the central horizontal one forming the hand grip.

The handle across the central boss may have provided one means of carrying the shield but a horseman, who held the reins in the left hand as well, must have been provided with a second handle and perhaps additional straps to support it. Sculptural evidence supports this view but does not clarify the particular method used; nor, to date, does the archaeological record.

A considerable number of early Imperial shield designs are known to us from monumental evidence, and some more or less

LEFT The stages of painting the cavalry shield. I drew the scorpion first from a photo of the shield on Trajan's Column; the Roman sculptor obviously knew his arachnids. The blue background of the shield was painted next; then I painted the four scorpions on to this. You can see how this was done by following the progressive development of the design round the shield. In a similar manner you can follow the painting of the brass edging round from the raw modelling putty at the top to the dry-brushed and highlighted section at bottom right.

credible attempts have been made to attribute particular designs to known units of the Roman army. We still know practically nothing about the colours of these designs, though there is good evidence that the backs of certain shields were coloured a dull red. There is a useful Wargames Research Group publication that summarises and illustrates most of what is known or speculated on this subject (see Bibliography).

It was not difficult to reconstruct the design on the face of the hexagonal shield from Trajan's Column. The bottom of the shield was obscured, but the three visible scorpions suggested that a fourth must have completed the design. I decided to consider the colours of the shield in relation to the group as a whole. Most of the trappings of the horse and clothing of the cavalryman were to be in the red, brown, russet and beige range of colours. There would be little or no blue; once I decided that it would make a good contrast to use this colour for the background of the shield, the scorpions just had to be yellow. Painting the scorpion design was really no different to painting medieval heraldry, and you can see how this was done in the accompanying photographs.

There has been a shift of opinion lately about the colour of the tunics of Roman

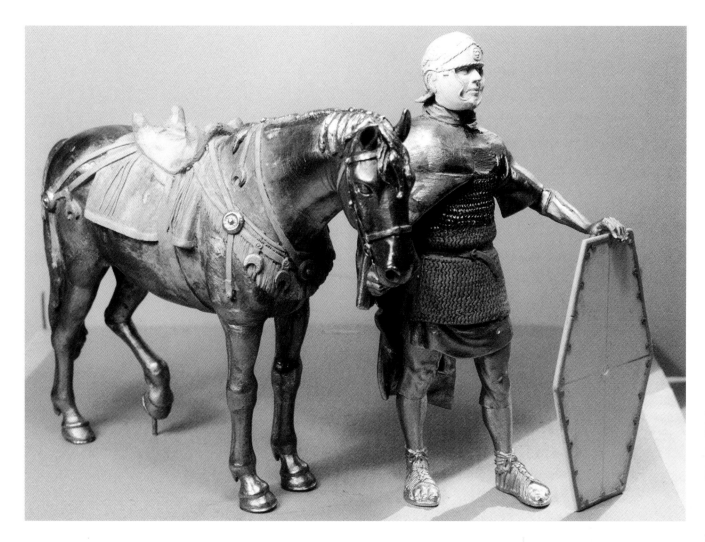

soldiers, which were traditionally believed to have been red. Recent scholarship suggests that they were 'white', presumably meaning undyed self-coloured wool. With this in mind I decided that my cavalryman ought to be up to date, so I gave him a white tunic. It would be interesting to see the effect of this colour, though I thought that it would have to be several tones darker than a tennis dress to maintain credibility.

MORE WORK ON THE FIGURE

The horse was ready, the base was cut out, and I had the photos from Vindolanda. A package arrived from Rendal and I opened it with trepidation. It was the head; it was good, crisply detailed, and about the right size - or was it? I fixed it quickly in place and weighed it up from every angle; was it too big? The temptation to fiddle about with it was so great that I couldn't resist it. I had a go at it with my knife - just a bit off here and there, he'll never notice, there, that's better... I glued it in place and heaved a sigh of relief.

The cavalryman's cloak suggested the miserable weather of Northern Britain, and I planned to model a puddle of water on the base to further enhance the effect. I had hoped that there would be a minimum of conversion work on the figure, but found that I had to remodel part of the cloak when I altered the right arm to hold the horse's reins. The biggest job, as the metal was very hard, was cutting away the well-modelled but unwanted military belts along with some fringed edging to the mail shirt. I ended up by removing the bottom of this entirely as it was easier to remodel this area completely than to try to retain any of the original detail.

I used the hilt of the *gladius* from the infantry kit to make the longer-bladed *spatha* carried by the auxiliary cavalry, then glued this in place on the right hip. (This Roman peculiarity is much discussed by people who can't understand how the sword was drawn from the right side, but the contemporary sculptural evidence is quite clear on the point - e.g. see T. Flavius Bassus's tombstone.) The mail shirt was remodelled in one session using the method described in Chapter 1, and I managed to add most of the sword belt at the same time.

ABOVE The 80mm horse and the 90mm cavalryman with Rendal's new head are brought together for the first time to assess how successfully they work together. Rendal has modelled the head in white superfine Milliput; my own preference is for the yellow-grey standard grade, which you can see has been used extensively on the model.

When the kit first arrived I was rather surprised that the main component was the cloak, and at first I considered discarding it to show off more of the armour. Then I came across an illustration of the *paenula* or hooded cloak by Ron Embleton in *Hadrian's Wall in the*

Days of the Romans. The passage above read 'everyone, civilians and soldiers, wore the paenula at all times apart from a few summer months'. Well, I couldn't argue with that, so I left the cloak alone and added a puddle of water to the groundwork to go with it.

MODELLING THE SETTING

From my trip to Vindolanda I had a good photograph of a section of Hadrian's Wall complete with a reconstructed turret, and this was to be the basis of a simple setting. I scanned the photo into my computer and enlarged it to the appropriate size, then printed the image and mounted it on card. The hill and sky in the background of the print-out were then cut away to leave the Wall in profile; a more dramatic skyscape would be inserted behind this to give depth to the scene.

Next I built up an area of simple groundwork on a plywood base using card and textured filler. Some extra detail was added with Milliput, particularly round the horse's hooves so that they were bedded into the groundwork. There was a deep ditch in front of the Roman Wall for most of its length, and this was suggested by moving the photographic backdrop some distance back from the base.

APPENDIX

APPENDIX A
SUPPLIERS OF BOOKS & MATERIALS

Heraldry Today, Parliament Piece, Ramsbury nr. Marlborough, Wilts SN8 2QH. Publishers and suppliers of new and scarcer books on heraldry and allied subjects; catalogue available.

Ken Trotman Ltd., Unit 11, 135, Ditton Walk, Cambridge CB5 8PY. Catalogue of military books, new publications and a good selection of rare and hard to come by Ancient and Medieval titles.

Fred W.Aldus, PO Box 135, 37 Lever St., Manchester M60 1UX. Supplier of craft materials including sheet pewter.

Alec Tiranti, 70 High St., Theale, Reading, Berks RG7 5AR. Mail order sculptors' catalogue; mould-making materials and instructions.

Squires Model & Craft Tools, 100 London Rd., Bognor Regis, West Sussex PO 21 1DD. Practically everything the modeller could ever desire, illustrated in a comprehensive 330-page mail order catalogue.

Hobby's Annual, W.Hobby Ltd., Knight's Hill Square, London SE27 0HH. Interesting and useful 260-page mail order catalogue of craft and modelmaking tools and materials.

MODEL KITS

Most manufacturers have some ancient or medieval figures available, and some produce them almost exclusively, but I don't propose to list them all here. There are a wealth of well-sculpted ancient and medieval models available in a variety of scales from manufacturers large and small, though there are very few model shops in the UK nowadays which carry a good stock of figure kits. Modelling magazines such as *Military Modelling* carry advertising and reviews of new products, and most firms produce a catalogue and offer a direct mail order service. In addition the Internet is becoming increasingly popular as a means of introducing products to a wide audience.

APPENDIX B
MODEL PHOTOGRAPHY

The photographs which illustrate the model projects in this book were all taken in a similar way using simple equipment. I used a semi-automatic Minolta SG-1 Single Lens Reflex (SLR) camera with a standard 50mm lens, which I keep mounted on a tripod at all times as a studio camera. This will only focus down to about 0.45m, so to allow me to close in on the subject I use a Hoya +1 screw-on magnifying lens as a first step; this allows me to fill the frame with an 80mm mounted figure. For closer work I use a set of three Minolta Auto Extension Tubes which fit between the body of the camera and the lens. If all three tubes are fitted a postage stamp will fill the frame, but if you get too close to the subject it becomes difficult to light, and tiny surface imperfections become too noticeable. Neither of these fittings have any effect on the exposure - there is no need to alter this to compensate for them as they do it automatically. Lighting is everything in model photography; I use two Phillips No.1 Photoflood bulbs and light the subject variably from the front. There is no formula; the angles differ every time and inevitably there is some trial and error involved.

APPENDIX C

BIBLIOGRAPHY

Books are tools, every bit as much as files and pliers, and like hand tools they vary widely in their usefulness and in the frequency with which you will use them. Practically all the books included in this Bibliography have been consulted in some way or other during the preparation of this book. The titles included have been selected for their usefulness to modellers; however, a fair proportion of them will inevitably be out of print. Not all the books we buy turn out to be as useful as we think at the time of purchase, and some inevitably end up in the second hand bookshop; but this is all part of the process of building a library. Sometimes an otherwise worthless book is worth keeping for a few of its illustrations alone, and these have been noted as an aside.

Some books use out-of-context illustrations simply as space fillers; thus a late 15th century manuscript drawing will be inserted into the text and captioned misleadingly as if it were a contemporary depiction of an event in the mid-14th century. In this way the battle of Crécy may be illustrated by a drawing of soldiers in the armour of the Wars of the Roses. This is worse than useless, it is actively misleading; so readers and modellers who are not yet experienced enough to tell the difference at a glance should study the more serious sources carefully to train their eye.

PAINTING MODEL FIGURES

Bill Horan's Military Modelling Masterclass, Windrow & Greene (now available Osprey Publishing), ISBN 1 872004 09 1

HERALDRY

Lyn Armstrong, *The Siege of Caerlaverock Castle, AD 1300*, Lynda Armstrong Designs, ISBN1 902667 01 8

Pete Armstrong, *The Battle of Bannockburn, June 1314*, Lynda Armstrong Designs, ISBN 1 902667 02 6

Pete Armstrong, *The Battles of Stirling Bridge and Falkirk,1297-1298*, Lynda Armstrong Designs, ISBN 1 902667 00 X

Thos. Coveney, *Heraldic Banners of The Wars of the Roses*, Freezywater Publications, 13 Rochester Drive, Lincoln

J. Foster, *Some Feudal Coats of Arms* (1902), reprinted as *The Dictionary of Heraldry* (1989), ISBN 1 85170 309 8

J. Foster, *Some Feudal Lords and Their Seals*, Crecy Books (reprint 1984), ISBN 0 947554 01 7

Stephen Friar (ed.), *A New Dictionary of Heraldry*, Alphabooks, ISBN 0 906670 44 6

W.E.Hampton, *Memorials of The Wars of the Roses*, The Richard III Society, ISBN 0 904893 03 0

Cecil R.Humphery-Smith, *Anglo Norman Armory Two*, IHGS (1984), ISBN 0 9504879 8 8

Jonathan Jones, *Standards, Badges and Livery Colours of The Wars of the Roses*, Freezywater Publications, 13 Rochester Drive, Lincoln

W.R.MacDonald, *Scottish Armorial Seals* (Edinburgh 1904)

Rosemary Pinches & Anthony Wood, *A European Armorial*, Heraldry Today, ISBN 0 900455 13 6

C.W.Scott-Giles, *Shakespeare's Heraldry*, Heraldry Today, ISBN 0 900455 12 8

Sir Anthony Wagner (ed.), *Aspilogia II, Rolls of Arms of Henry III*,The Society of Antiquaries (London 1967)

Geoffrey Wheeler, *The Battle of Tewkesbury 1471*, Freezywater Publications, 13 Rochester Drive, Lincoln

Terence Wise, *Medieval Heraldry*, Osprey Men-At-Arms Series 99, ISBN 0 85045 348 8

Les Blasons des 24 Grands Matîres de l'Ordre du Temple, Délires 1995 (picture cards), ISBN 2 911072 02 2

THE ROMANS & THE DARK AGES

Phil Barker, *The Armies and Enemies of Imperial Rome*, Wargames Research Group publication

M.L.Bishop & J.C.N.Coulston, *Roman Military Equipment*, Batsford, ISBN 0 7134 7627 3

Peter Connolly, *The Cavalryman*, The Roman World Series, Oxford University Press, ISBN 0 19 910424 7

Ronald Embleton & Frank Graham, *Hadrian's Wall in the Days of the Romans*, Frank Graham, ISBN 0 85983 177 9

Daniel Peterson, *The Roman Legions Recreated in Colour Photographs*, Windrow & Greene (now available Crowood Press), ISBN 1 872004 06 7

H.Russell Robinson, *The Armour of Imperial Rome*, Arms & Armour Press, SBN 85368 219 4; and Charles Scribner's Sons, New York, ISBN 0 684 13956 1

Michael Simkins, *The Roman Army from Caesar to Trajan*, Osprey Men-at-Arms Series 46, ISBN 0 85045 528 6

Martin Windrow & Angus McBride, *Imperial Rome at War*, Concord Publications Company, ISBN 962 361 608 2

B.Nurmann, C.Schulze & T.Verhülsdonk, *The Vikings Recreated in Colour Photographs*, Windrow & Greene (now available Crowood Press), ISBN 1 86126 289 2

R.Ewart Oakeshott, *Dark Age Warrior*, Lutterworth Press, ISBN 0 7188 2079 7

Dominic Tweddle, *The Coppergate Helmet*, Cultural Resource Management, Jorvik Viking Centre, York

Richard Underwood, *Anglo-Saxon Weapons & Warfare*, Tempus, ISBN 07524 1412 7

MEDIEVAL ARMOUR, DRESS & WEAPONS

Claude Blair, *European Armour circa 1066 to circa 1700*, Batsford, ISBN 0 7134 0729 8

Lionello Georgio Boccia, *Le Armature di S.Maria Delle Grazie di Curtatone di Mantova e L'Armatura Lombarda del'400*, Bramante Editrice

Arthur Richard Dufty, *European Armour in The Tower of London*, HMSO

David Edge & John Miles Paddock, *Arms & Armour of the Medieval Knight*, Defoe Publishing, ISBN 1 870981 00 6

Gerry Embleton & John Howe, *The Medieval Soldier: 15th Century Campaign Life Recreated in Colour Photographs*, Windrow & Greene (now available Crowood Press), ISBN 1 85915 036 5

Ian Heath, *The Armies of the Middle Ages*, Volume 1, Wargames Research Group publication

Ann Hyland, *The Medieval Warhorse from Byzantium to the Crusades*, Grange Books, ISBN 1 85627 990 1

R.Ewart Oakeshott, *A Knight and His Armour*, Lutterworth Press

R.Ewart Oakeshott, *The Sword in the Age of Chivalry*, Lutterworth Press

Sir Ralph Payne-Gallwey, *The Crossbow*, Bramhall House (New York)

Eduard Wagner, *Medieval Costume, Armour and Weapons 1350-1450*, Hamlyn

Terence Wise & Gerry Embleton, *The Wars of the Roses*, Osprey Men-at-Arms Series 145, ISBN 0 85045 520 0

MISCELLANEOUS

Muriel Clayton, *Catalogue of Rubbings of Brasses and Incised Slabs*, Victoria and Albert Museum, HMSO, ISBN 0 11 290087 9

W.Ellenberger, H.Baum & H.Dittrich, *An Atlas of Animal Anatomy for Artists*, Dover, ISBN 0 486 20082 5

Harold G.Leask, *Irish Castles and Castellated Houses*, Dundalgan Press, Dundalk

Eadweard Muybridge, *Horses and Other Animals in Motion*, Dover, ISBN 0 486 24911 5

Nikolaus Pevsner, *The Buildings of England Series*, Penguin (volumes for each county)

Roy Porter's Model Buildings Masterclass, Windrow & Grene (now available Osprey Publishing), ISBN 1 85915 063 2